SEX EDUCATION FOR TEENS

ANSWERS YOU SEEK, FOR THE QUESTIONS YOU'RE TOO SHY TO ASK

The Comprehensive Guide to Understand
Sexuality, Puberty, Relationships
and Digital Safety

Elena Bennett

Thank you for your purchase

SCAN THIS QR CODE BELOW
to get your **FREE BONUS BOOK** and
master essential life skills in less than 48 hours!

Why You Shouldn't Miss This Bonus and What You'll Learn:

- **Mastering Personal Finance**: Essentials of budgeting, saving, and smart spending.
- **Time Management**: Prioritize tasks, set goals, and maintain an organized schedule.
- **Effective Communication**: Active listening, clear expression, and conflict resolution.
- **Health and Wellness**: Balanced diet, physical activity, and mental well-being.
- **Critical Thinking**: Informed decisions, creativity, and problem-solving skills.
- **Digital Literacy**: Protect personal information, navigate social media, use productivity tools.

ELENA BENNETT

ESSENTIAL LIFE SKILLS *for teens*

20 24

YOUR GUIDE TO THRIVING IN ADULTHOOD

Redeem your FREE bonus

TABLE OF CONTENTS

PREFACE

Dear Reader,

I'm Elena Bennett, the author of "Sex Education for Teens - Answers You Seek, For the Questions You're Too Shy to Ask". I'd like to start by saying how pleased I am to meet you and how honored I am that my book is now in your hands. I truly believe that accurate information, openly shared, is profoundly empowering, and that's why I'm thrilled that you've taken the idea of learning about your health, your body, and the dynamics of relationships seriously enough to have picked up this book.

Introducing such a guide wasn't an impulsive endeavor; it entails the amalgamation of expertise, authentic experiences, insights, and an-depth understanding of the field. Reflecting a fine balance between scientific understanding and accessible language, this guide is the result of meticulous efforts focused on breeding substantial change.

In this book, you'll find countless topics about adolescence and puberty, the changes your body goes through, the emotions that accompany these changes, and every other question that you've contemplated but hesitated to ask. To make the book truly helpful, we will navigate through the territories of intimacy, sexual health, consent and respect, the secure usage of the digital world, and, importantly, the aspects that entail healthy relationships.

One of the book's unique features is its focus on empowering you with the information to make informed decisions about your sexual health and relationships. My hope is that this book helps you understand the intricacies of your body, its functions, changes, and responses. More importantly, it's designed to help you understand that each person's journey through puberty and into adulthood is as unique as they are themselves.

This guide is also an open acknowledgment of your fears, questions, and the pressure you may feel, understanding that being a teenager in today's world is not easy. The digital landscape, with its vast potential, can also lead to new pressures and expectations; and therefore, some sections of this guide deal explicitly with these aspects.

This book is your companion, but, like a wise friend who respects your feelings and decisions. The voice throughout this guide empathizes with your curiosity, questions, and apprehensions. No judgment, only understanding — that's my promise to you.

In our society, discussions about sex and sexual health are often shrouded in silence or embarrassment, contributing to the spread of myths and misinformation. This guide aims to break those barriers and initiate an open conversation on sex education.

My parting advice to you as you start your journey with this book is to approach it with an open heart and mind. Remember, the quest for knowledge is a beautiful journey, one that empowers and liberates you.

Embark on this journey of discovery, understanding, and empathy as we strive to make sense of an essential phase of life - Teenage.

Warm regards,
Elena Bennett

INTRODUCTION

| OPENING WORDS: THE JOURNEY OF DISCOVERY

Welcome, dear reader, to your journey of discovery. A journey that you have taken the first step toward, guided by your curiosity and the need to understand the myriad changes that you're undergoing and will continue to experience in the years ahead. A sincere congratulations! Taking this step is a demonstration of your fortitude and intelligence — it says a lot about who you are and who you are set to become.

Remember, no journey follows a straight path, and there will be ebbs and flows along the way. The same is true for this journey of understanding your body, emotions, and the intricate dynamics of relationships that go hand in hand with becoming a sexual being. Change is a constant companion of adolescence and puberty, manifesting in ways that are biological, psychological, and emotional. It can be exhilarating, confusing, and even intimidating at times.

Here's the important truth: change is natural. Each individual change is a single thread in the grand tapestry of growth and development. This doesn't make pubertal changes any less frustrating or puzzling, but realizing that you're not alone and that these changes are universal can make them slightly less overwhelming.

This book, your new companion, is designed to walk you through this complex journey, answering questions, dispelling myths, and fostering understanding. You might have been bombarded with a lot of information or misinformation about these topics, from peers, from the internet, or even from overheard adult conversations. It's essential to remember that everything you've heard may not be accurate or applicable to you; that's where this guide comes in.

First things first, it's okay to have questions that you're too shy or embarrassed to ask. These naturally arising questions are part of your growth and part of becoming an informed adult. From our perspective, no question is too trivial or "stupid" — if it matters to you, it matters to us. We're here not only to answer your questions but also to encourage them. Each query paves the path to knowledge and understanding.

This guide is created to help you navigate your thoughts and concerns effectively. You might find it worthwhile to have a notebook handy while reading this book, allowing you to jot down any thoughts, feelings, or additional questions that arise. And yes, questions will come up, and that's completely okay! Consider it a sign of your intellectual curiosity and critical thinking.

This journey that we're sharing is about education. In its truest sense, education is about understanding the world around us so that we can navigate it efficiently and thrive within it. That's precisely what we aim to do here— help you understand the world of adolescence, puberty, sexual health, and relationships. The knowledge you gain will be your compass, guiding you securely through the labyrinth of teen years.

We are at the start of a remarkable, inspiring endeavor. As the saying goes, "The journey of a thousand miles begins with a single step." You have taken that crucial first step by choosing this guide. Now, I invite you, with open arms and a steadfast commitment, to embark on this journey of discovery, understanding, and empowerment together. Let's navigate through these transformative years with courage, curiosity, and compassion, paving the way to informed choices, healthy relationships, and ownership of your sexual health.

HOW TO NAVIGATE THIS GUIDE: TOOLS FOR UNDERSTANDING

If adolescence were a country, then puberty would undoubtedly be its most populated state. It's a shared journey of transformation travelled by every teenager. Yet, despite its universal nature, puberty is a deeply personal and varied experience for every individual. It's the span where crucial physical developments coincide with shifting emotions and growing awareness of oneself as a sexual being.

Let's start by setting the scene. You wake up one morning, and there it is — the first overt sign that puberty has initiated its visit. Perhaps it's a voice that breaks rabbit-like without warning or hair sprouting in new places, or possibly a peek of a first pimple. Suddenly, you're on this exciting yet somewhat daunting path of transformations — a road with several milestones, detours, and promising horizons.

The idea behind this roadmap is not to predict every twist and turn – that would be impossible given the diverse range of puberty experiences. Instead, the roadmap of puberty outlines fundamental changes that most teenagers undergo. Think of it as a general guide, a broad sketch of what lies ahead. The finer details you'll fill in yourself, with your own colors, based on your unique experiences.

The roadmap of puberty is one that extends over several years, typically beginning around ages 9-12 for girls and 11-14 for boys. However, this can vary significantly. There's no "right" age to start puberty. It's a process that graciously heeds to its own timeline, refusing to be hurried or slowed down by societal pressures or expectations.

Even within the framework of puberty, the order of changes might vary. For some, growth spurts happen early on; for others, it might lag behind other developments. Some girls might get their periods before the full development of their breasts. Some boys might notice their first facial hair before their voice deepens. The sequence of these changes is as unique as you are.

Puberty is a chronicle of physical growth and change that prepares the body for sexual reproduction. Among these changes are those that you can clearly see — the growth spurts, the development of primary and secondary sexual traits such as breasts, testes, and pubic hair. Others are more subtle, like the surge of hormones silently choreographing these remarkable alterations.

Puberty is also an emotional journey, directly related to the rampaging hormones that don't just affect your body, but your emotions and your brain too. Emotionally, you might find yourself on a rollercoaster of feeling self-conscious one moment, angry the next, and then unexpectedly euphoric. You might start finding someone attractive or become interested in dating. This newfound emotional depth is part of becoming an adult and developing more complex emotional relationships.

Over the course of this guide, we'll delve into these changes in more detail. Our exploration of puberty will not be limited to the physical aspects but also the subsequent emotional shifts, perceptions, impacts on self-image, and more.

Lastly, but most importantly, embarking on this roadmap of puberty is to understand that each person's journey through puberty is unique. The speed at which changes happen, the way they manifest, and how you feel about them varies. This variation is perfectly normal. Stomachs knot with anxiety if you think you're behind your peers or ahead of them in this journey, but there's no schedule that puberty adheres to.

Remember, the roadmap of puberty isn't a race, it's a journey of growth, of morphing into the astonishing adults that you will become. It's about getting to know yourself better- physically and emotionally. So, fasten your seatbelts, hold on to the spirit of inquiry, and join us as we embark on this fascinating journey through puberty, marking one of the most transformative phases of life.

DIALOGUE AND EDUCATION: THE PILLARS OF SEX KNOWLEDGE

The funny thing about conversations around sex and sexuality is how they're both ubiquitous and yet strangely silent. Sex is discussed everywhere—in Lady Gaga songs, in advertisements promising attraction, in movies that play out grand romantic stories. Yet, when it comes to discussing sex transparently, especially in the context of sex education, the subject is often glossed over, ignored, or replaced with coded language.

The need for open, insightful conversations about sex is perhaps nowhere more felt than in the tumultuous years of adolescence. Without reliable information and safe avenues for discussion, myths and misconceptions about sex readily bloom in the fertile grounds of curiosity and misinformation that often pervade teenage spaces.

ELENA BENNETT

That's where the dual pillars of dialogue and education come in, and what this book stands firmly upon. Armed with these tools, we'll strive to dismantle the myths, unmask the mysteries, and bring out the realities of the sexual journey you find yourself on.

Dialogue—the very word reflects a back-and-forth, a sharing of perspectives, an exchange of understanding. We encourage a dialogue not just between us through this book and you as a reader, but also within yourself and with others.

A dialogue with oneself is crucial on this path of self-discovery. Identify your feelings, ask yourself questions, and navigate your way through finding the answers. As we discuss various topics in this book—such as self-identity, intimacy, consent, and digital media safety—we hope to stimulate this internal dialogue.

In terms of dialogues with others, they can occur on multiple levels. On one side of the spectrum, having open, non-judgmental family dialogues can be instrumental in ensuring that teenagers receive correct information and emotional support about concerns related to sexual health. Friendships can also serve to provide frank, empathic exchanges on various sexual health topics. However, peer discussions, although vital for sharing experiences and advice, should always be complemented by information from credible sources.

A dialogue also opens doors for a community or school-based discussion. Adolescents stand to gain from interactive sessions, workshops, or forums where trained professionals communicate sexual health information in relatable ways. You might be surprised how much easier it is to discuss sex when it's approached as a medical and social topic—and not a secretive or taboo subject.

The other pillar, education, is a torchlight in the sometimes confusing labyrinth of teenage years. Accurate knowledge can dispel fears, equip you for decision-making, and empower you to respect both your boundaries and those of others.

Let's address the most essential question here: What is 'sex education'? Is it just about the act of sex itself? A resounding 'no' is the answer. Sex education is not just about sexual intercourse or reproduction. It is a comprehensive approach that deals with a range of topics that are often interconnected. It covers biological aspects like puberty, sexual health issues such as STIs and contraception, emotional aspects such as intimacy and body image, social aspects like peer pressure, and the concept of consent.

Moreover, sex education weaves in the thread of respect throughout its fabric. It gives due regard to managing emotions, respecting personal and others' boundaries, understanding the illegal and unethical aspects of sex, such as assault and harassment. It also looks at sex in the broader societal perspective, helping you understand your sexual rights and responsibilities.

Under the beacon of these fundamental constructs of dialogue and education, this book's content is mapped out. Each chapter will delve into various areas of adolescent sexual health, sparking insights and hopefully kindling the curiosity to learn more. In an environment rife with misinformation and misunderstanding, dialogue and education are the fulcrjets to bring forth clarity and comfort in getting to know the sexual aspect of one's identity. If these pages do more than inform and spur conversations within and around you, this book would have served its purpose well. So, let's leap on this rollercoaster of discovery, understanding, and maturity together—understanding that learning is constant and that every question matters. Because when it comes to sex education, knowledge is indeed power.

CHAPTER 1
THE BODY'S JOURNEY

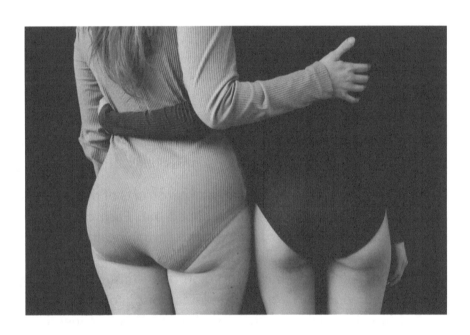

| THE ROADMAP OF PUBERTY: WHAT LIES AHEAD

As we begin our journey through adolescence and puberty, it's important to remember that no two paths are the same. The multitude of changes that occur during these transformative years fall on a wide spectrum, a profoundly personal timeline that cannot and should not be compared with someone else's. Every person's experiences are unique to them. These distinct changes and experiences are what make us the individuals we become, and there is as much beauty in these differences as there is in our shared experiences.

The roadmap of puberty is one such collective adventure bathed in varied hues. The sprawling landscape of adolescence is marked by physical, emotional, and social alterations, typically kicking off around ages 9-12 for females and 11-14 for males. This age range is an average estimate, and it's crucial to understand that there is an extensive range of what's considered normal. Puberty has its timeline, which depends on a combination of hereditary, nutritional, environmental, and other factors.

The onset of puberty is like striking a bio-physical gong, sending ripple effects that manifest as various changes in the body. You might notice your height and weight fluctuating courtesy of growth spurts. Simultaneously, primary and secondary sexual traits begin to develop. For girls, these changes may include the development of breasts, start of menstruation, and growth of pubic hair, while boys might notice the enlargement of their testicles and penis, voice deepening, and increased muscle mass.

Keep in mind the cultural sketch of changes is broad; the finer detailing varies for each individual. Some might notice changes earlier than their peers or even later. The timeline and spectrum of changes that take place during puberty differ in every teenager's life.

But what triggers these developments? Who flips the proverbial switch triggering puberty? That responsibility falls on an endocrine gland located at the base of the brain – the pituitary gland, often hailed as the maestro of your endocrine orchestra. It kickstarts puberty by increasing the production of two essential hormones— gonadotropin-releasing hormone (GnRH) and gonadotropins. These hormones stimulate the testes in boys and ovaries in girls to release sex hormones, which, in turn, initiate the cascade of physical and sexual maturation.

While the physical changes are more visible and often talked about during puberty, a whirlwind of emotional changes accompanies them. From heightened self-awareness and curiosity about bodies to the newfound emotional depth—it's indeed a rollercoaster ride. These changes are a significant part of puberty and are influenced by those silent conductors, hormones, which also affect your feelings and emotions. The emotions that you start experiencing during this period, from mood swings to a deeper capacity for empathy and complicated emotions like romantic attraction, are all part of growing up.

However, emotions aside, one of the challenges that adolescents often face while navigating the roadmap of puberty involves body image. The rapid changes occurring in the body can sometimes lead to feelings of awkwardness and insecurity. It's essential to foster a positive body image, to see and appreciate your body for the magical, hardworking entity it is—providing you with the means to explore, experience, and interact with the world around you.

Embracing the journey through puberty means making peace with the changes and accepting them as parts of you. Remember, there's no need to hasten or decelerate these changes; let your body follow its natural course, its pace. Trust that it knows what it's doing, even if you aren't fully sure yourself yet.

There can be intimidating bends, bumps, and detours on the roadmap of puberty. But by virtue of reading this guide, you're already well equipped with reliable information and a spirit of inquiry to navigate them skillfully. In the end, the journey through adolescence isn't about arriving on the other side as quickly as possible, but embracing the path itself, for every experience enriches us and contributes to the person we're becoming. Let's make the journey through puberty indeed a 'path of discovery,' one that leads to understanding, acceptance, and self-love.

| THE CHEMISTRY OF CHANGE: HORMONES AT WORK

So, what exactly lights the fire of puberty? What sets off this intricate series of changes that transform a child into an adult? The answer lies in the incredible world of hormones. Like silent messengers, these chemicals are produced in one part of the body and travel to others to regulate essential functions and maintain the body's internal equilibrium. In other words, hormones are at the center stage, conducting the symphony of physical and emotional changes that occur during puberty.

It all begins with the brain. Nestled at the bottom of this complex organ is a small pea-sized gland known as the pituitary gland. Long before the first signs of puberty become visible, the pituitary gland awakens from its slumber. It releases the Gonadotropin-Releasing Hormone (GnRH), which travels to another part of the brain that commands the pituitary to start producing the gonadotropins — two hormones known as Luteinizing Hormone (LH) and Follicle-stimulating Hormone (FSH). Gonadotropins act as the starting gun for the race that is puberty, setting the pace for the exciting journey of maturation.

The gonadotropins make their way to the gonads: ovaries in females and testes in males. This is where their real work begins. In saunters Testosterone, the prominent male sex hormone. It is produced in the testes (under the influence of the LH) and is predominantly responsible for changes such as enlargement of the testes and penis, muscle development, deepening voice, and the growth of facial and pubic hair in boys.

Meanwhile, in the ovaries of girls, the FSH whispers the mandate to start producing estrogen. This female hormone choreographs the onset of menstruation, the development of breasts, and the widening of hips along with other physical changes. It is noteworthy that while estrogen and testosterone are designated female and male hormones, both hormones exist in people of all genders, just in different amounts.

But the wonder of hormones doesn't stop there. They're also the unseen puppeteers of emotional fluctuations during puberty. The flux of hormones doesn't merely bring about physical changes. They interweave into your brain structure, influencing emotions, mood and even stretching to the realm of mental health. Some days might seem like an emotional whirlwind. Mood swings, heightened sensitivity, more profound emotionality and pronounced feelings of self-consciousness can all be attributed to the hormonal changes that occur during puberty.

Beneath all these changes, another hormone, a quiet agent named progesterone, starts to play an increasingly important role in girls' bodies, preparing the uterus for possible pregnancy and playing a key role in the monthly menstrual cycle.

This delightful hormonal ballet happens in every human, rhythmically guiding each person through their individual journey of puberty. But, it's important to remember that the hormonal journey isn't picture-perfect or constant. Hormonal levels can ebb and flow, altering the pace of the changes that carry you on waves from the shores of childhood to those of adolescence.

While this complex interplay of hormones might seem somewhat intimidating, understanding this chemistry can empower you to better comprehend your body's changes. It can also help instill a sense of patience and kindness toward yourself. Mood swings, acne, voice cracks — they're all part of this vast hormonal pageant that is puberty.

Keep in mind, this hormonal orchestra is your body's way of growing, of transforming, of becoming. It's not something to be rushed, resisted, or resented. The hormonal path is much like a river carving a path through a canyon, leaving behind marvellous natural wonders in its wake. As the hormones flute away, chiselling out the evolved version of you, take a moment to marvel at the silent symphony your body conducts—the chemistry of change at incredible work.

| EMBRACING SELF-LOVE: BODY IMAGE AND ACCEPTANCE

As we navigate the roadmap of puberty and traverse the hormonal landscape, a parallel journey unfolds—one that often gets less attention but is just as crucial. This journey is the internal voyage towards acceptance and self-love, especially in relation to our bodies.

As adolescents, acceptance is among the most challenging personal projects. At a time when the body seems to be its own maestro, it can feel like you're a passenger in your own life. Your body alters in ways that can sometimes be strange and disconcerting. These physical changes paired with hormonal influences can lead to heightened self-consciousness, increased scrutiny of your appearance and, at times, blows to your self-esteem. This emotional whirlwind can dwindle the tenderness you hold for your evolving body.

It is vital to remember that puberty isn't a cookie-cutter process where one size fits all. It's a multi-colored spectrum where each color shines with different hues. Differences are the norm during puberty. Some might grow taller faster. Some might have sudden acne flares. Some could gain weight quicker than their peers. Everyone changes at their own rhythm. It's this unique rhythm that contributes to the diverse array of human bodies we see around us.

It's natural to have mixed feelings about your changing body. For example, some girls might feel uncomfortable or embarrassed as their breasts develop, while boys might feel awkward when their voice breaks unexpectedly. However, understanding that these changes aren't designed to fulfill beauty standards or to compete with others, but purely to prepare your body for adulthood, can help shift perspective.

Instead of seeing these changes as awkward or embarrassing, remind yourself that they are mere signs of your body marvelously preparing you for adulthood. When we accept these changes as natural, expected phases of growth—not discords to be hastily tuned—we turn the key to acceptance and self-love.

Comparison is often seen as a thief of joy and, unfortunately, a largely unbidden one during adolescence. The desire to compare might feel intensified by an army of external messages from magazines, television shows, social media, and movies selling an unattainable, airbrushed picture of 'perfection.' Do your best not to surrender to these pressures. Remind yourself that these beautifully diverse changes aren't about achieving standardized beauty, but about gearing your incredible body for the adulthood lined up for you.

Unshakeable self-love starts with acceptance. Resist the urge to shrink into the mold of societal expectations. Celebrate uniqueness. Encourage diversity. Each one of us is different, and that's what makes us extrordinary. Body acceptance isn't a switch that can be instantaneously flipped on, it's a journey with ups, downs, and winding paths.

Self-love is also about taking care of your body. It means ensuring you're eating nutritious meals and staying physically active, no matter what shape your body is taking. It means getting enough sleep – a necessity, not luxury, during adolescence. It's about practicing basic hygiene and taking time to tune out and relax. Treating your body with care tells your subconscious that you are worthy of nurturing and love.

Lastly, remember to be patient with yourself. As the waves of change make their way to the shore of self-acceptance, it's okay to take time to explore your feelings about your body. It's okay to reach out to trusted adults or peers with your concerns. It's okay to seek professional help if body anxiety starts to overwhelm you.

As we forge ahead on this journey of self-discovery, think of puberty as a bridge between childhood and adulthood. It's the architect of the adult you will be, the designer shaping you with strokes of natural wisdom. So, do yourself a favor. As you cross this bridge, walk with your head held high and heart filled with self-acceptance, knowing that the person who greets you on the other side is someone you love wholeheartedly. After all, the journey to self-love begins with accepting change and blooming at your own pace.

Discovering Self: Gender and Orientation Exploration

As we journey together through the tumultuous yet fascinating terrain of puberty, we continue to observe, appreciate, and, hopefully, accept the rich tapestry of changes unfolding within us. Yet, amidst the physical and emotional vagaries, you may find yourself standing at the threshold of another intriguing realm of self-discovery—the exploration of your gender identity and sexual orientation.

Adolescence is like embarking on a quest, an inward venture to discover and understand your authentic self. It is during this period that many begin to ponder their identities and orientations, questioning where they fit in the spectra of gender and sexuality. This discovery process is deeply personal and unique to each individual, punctuated with questions, doubts, realizations, and acceptance.

Firstly, it's important to distinguish between biological sex, assigned at birth based on physical characteristics, and gender, a complex weave of societal roles, personal identification, and internal feelings. While sex revolves around male, female, and intersex, gender unfolds as a spectrum—from male and female to a vast range of identities and expressions including transgender, genderqueer, non-binary, genderfluid, and more. Remember, it's possible to feel aligned with your birth-assigned sex, to feel a divergence, or to even question it.

Parallel to gender, around puberty, you also start experiencing sexual attraction, sparking questions about sexual orientation—an integral aspect of human sexuality related to whom one is romantically or sexually attracted to. You might identify as heterosexual, homosexual, bisexual, asexual, pansexual, or prefer not to specify your sexual orientation. Like gender, sexual orientation isn't strictly categorical; it is, in reality, multifaceted and fluid for some.

You might ask, "but how do I know?" The truth is, there is no universal timeline or process to identify your gender identity or sexual orientation. It may start with questioning, with acknowledging what feels right and what doesn't, and subtly piecing together the facets of your identity like an intimate puzzle. Some may have strong convictions about their gender and orientation early in life, while others may need more time to explore, to understand.

The thrill and trepidation of self-discovery can be a mix of emotions. There might be periods of doubt, confusion, or even fear. Remember, it is okay to feel unsure, and it is absolutely fine to give yourself the time and space to understand better. This discovery process is not a race to a destination; it's about exploring your authentic self at your own pace.

This journey of self-discovery isn't solely solitary. Seek solace in trustworthy friends or supportive adults who can provide a listening ear and compassionate advice. Sometimes, articulating your feelings and thoughts can bring clarity and reassurance. If external resources are available and accessible to you, consider reaching out to LGBTQ+ organizations or support groups for information, guidance, and connection with others experiencing similar journeys.

Understanding the trajectories of gender and sexuality is a delicate task and one that is deeply personal. Dedicate kindness to yourself during this exploration. Embrace the exploration, even the uncertainty, for it is a testament to your individual growth. Your gender identity and sexual orientation are but pieces of the broader, beautiful puzzle that makes you, uniquely you.

The exploration of sexual orientation and gender identity during puberty is instrumental in fostering self-discovery and building a holistic understanding of oneself. As navigation continues through this intricate labyrinth of adolescence, remember that whatever identity or orientation aligns with your authentic self, whether it shadows society's norms or transcends them, is valid, is accepted, and is something to be celebrated. After all, the charm of humanity lies in its diversity — in acknowledging, respecting, and celebrating differences as vibrant threads weaving the rich tapestry of life. It's this vibrant tapestry that can collectively usher in a more understanding and accepting world.

WELLNESS AND CARE: PRIORITIZING YOUR PHYSICAL HEALTH

As we traverse the landscape of puberty and navigate our identity, one crucial aspect needs our keen attention – wellness and care. This topic might not grab headlines as much as explosive growth spurts or voice cracks, but it is a fact that self-care and respect for your growing body bear significantly on your journey through adolescence.

Adolescence is a whirlwind of changes, both physically and emotionally, making it all the more necessary to nurture your body with an approach geared towards wellness and self-care. It's not about vanity but about building a strong foundation for lifelong health and wellbeing.

First and foremost, eat well. Your body is growing and transforming at a pace like never before, necessitating a balanced diet. Fruits, vegetables, whole grains, proteins, and good fats should be your allies during these growing years. Equally important is drinking plenty of water to stay hydrated. Try to resist the constant lure of junk food, which though may satisfy your taste buds momentarily, does a disservice to your body in the long run.

Caring for your body also means making physical activity a regular part of your life. It doesn't have to be competitive sports, rather activities you enjoy. Riding a bike, dancing, hiking, or practicing yoga can all contribute to developing muscle strength, bone health, and overall physical fitness. Exercise also has a mood-enhancing effect—a bonus during the emotional roller coaster of adolescence.

Hygiene is another crucial aspect. As puberty hits, glands in the skin on your face and body can produce more oil, which may lead to acne. Regular cleansing to remove excess oil can help manage acne. Starting to use deodorants or antiperspirants can combat the stronger body odor that often accompanies puberty.

Sleep might not feel like a priority when you're juggling schoolwork, hobbies, social life, and coping with the changes of puberty. Yet, sufficient sleep is crucial for your physical health, cognitive function, and even mood regulation. Try to clock in an average of 8-10 hours of sleep a night. Remember, your body is working tirelessly during these transformative years; rest and rejuvenation are essential.

Take care of your mental health as well. Talk about your feelings—whether it's with friends, family, or mentors. Journaling can be a great outlet too. Remember, it's okay not to be okay all the time. Don't hesitate to reach out for help if feelings of sadness, worry, or irritability persist.

Lastly, don't undermine regular health check-ups. They are a good way to spot early signs of any health issue. Regular dental check-ups? Absolutely. Getting needed immunizations? Yes, those too. Taking care of your physical health enables you to be at the forefront of your life, ready to take on new challenges and experiences.

To be in the prime of your health, both physically and emotionally, is much more than just the absence of disease. It's a state of complete wellbeing where you're able to take part in life's delights wholeheartedly, while being resilient in the face of life's pressures. Prioritizing your physical health is the first crucial step towards achieving this. After all, the real journey of becoming isn't just about reaching a destination; it's about enjoying the journey itself—and you can best do that when you're feeling healthy, poised, and comfortable in your skin. So, here's to wellness, care, and a journey steeped in self-love. Be kind to your body, it's the only place you have to live in.

CHAPTER 2
EXPLORING INTIMACY

| UNRAVELING THE LAYERS OF INTIMACY

These rollercoaster years of adolescence, peppered with unprecedented changes, also unveil an entirely novel aspect of human connection – intimacy. As one starts discerning their identity and forming deeper relationships, the idea and exploration of intimacy become more prominent, holding hands with curiosity, apprehension and sometimes, exhilaration. Intimacy, however, isn't merely a one-dimensional concept capped by the physicality of a relationship. It's a composite of various layers, each with its significance and contribution towards forging meaningful relationships.

When we think of intimacy, most minds leap straight to its physical connotations – the territory of holding hands, hugging, kissing, and eventually, sexual involvement. However, equating intimacy exclusively with physical connections narrows its full breadth. Physical intimacy, while indeed an important facet, is merely one piece of the puzzle.

Remarkably, intimacy unravels its first layer through emotional ties—the backbone of human connections. The establishment of an emotional bond lays the foundation for true intimacy, the ability to share your feelings, fears, dreams, and insecurities with someone you trust and vice versa. Emotional intimacy is about understanding and being understood, about nurturing mutual respect for each other's feelings, and about entrusting someone with the vulnerable parts of yourself. Encouraging open, honest conversations— whether it's about your day, your fears, or your aspirations—fosters emotional intimacy, facilitating a safe space for both individuals to flourish.

Next to unveil itself is intellectual intimacy, built upon sharing ideas, engaging in thoughtful conversations, and respecting different perspectives. It's about appreciating the beauty of your partner's mind, curious about their thoughts, willing to learn from them, and vice versa. Embracing these intellectual exchanges fosters an environment rich in mutual understanding and respect.

Spiritual intimacy is another layer woven into the fabric of intimate relationships. It's about sharing beliefs, values, and ethical standards. It's about exploring life's deeper purpose together, charting out shared or individual spiritual journeys, and respecting the divergence in the paths you both might choose. This bond deepens mutual respect and nourishment, fostering a shared sense of peace and purpose.

Physical intimacy, the most commonly associated aspect of intimacy, is much more than engaging in sexual activities. It starts small – a brush of hands, a shared laugh, a comforting hug. It's about respecting and understanding each other's physical boundaries, being aware of each other's comfort levels, ensuring clear and enthusiastic consent before even approaching any physical boundaries.

It's important to realize that intimacy is not a switch flipped once you reach a certain age or milestone. It's a journey—sometimes slow and steady, other times a bit more complicated. The transformation from friends to intimate partners does not happen overnight. It's a gradual process requiring patience, built on trust, humility, and mutual respect.

Remember, interacting at these intimate levels is not only about sharing your narrative but also about listening and being there for the other person. And while navigating these layers of intimacy, it's crucial to ensure that the journey is mutual and consensual at every turn.

As we slowly unravel the layers of intimacy, it's essential to remember that the right to decide 'when' and 'if' lies with you. Prioritize your comfort and emotional readiness above societal impositions or pressures from peers. Your journey into exploring intimacy is your own—unique and personal. Therefore, enjoy each step, understanding that intimacy is a multifaceted expression of belief, warmth, connection, and respect. Let's demystify intimacy, delicately unraveling layers at our own pace, making sure that each thread weaves a tapestry of love, respect, and mutual consent.

EMOTIONS AND CONNECTIONS: THE HEART OF SEXUAL EXPERIENCE

In pop culture and media, the portrayal of sex often paints an image that's overly fixated on the physical, an act aimed at score-keeping or status-climbing. However, this perspective deprives the conversation of a vital aspect that forms the very heart of the sexual experience—emotions and connections. Understanding this emotional panorama is crucial in navigating sexual experiences healthily and respectfully.

Central to any sexual experience is not simply the act itself, but the emotional tapestry it's woven with. Emotional connections are significant contributors to sexual feelings. The warm flutter when you lock eyes, the electric spark held in an embrace, the rush of affectionate sentiment at a shared laugh—all of these stem from emotional bonding that, among many teenagers, often precedes physical desire.

The emotional underpinning shapes the nature of the sexual experience. Foremost, it encourages mutual respect and understanding. It empowers partners to communicate openly about their fears, aspirations, and expectations, encouraging a consensual interaction that is equally enjoyable for both. Bound by emotional understanding, sex becomes more than a physical connection; it transforms into an experience reflecting trust, consent, respect, and mutual pleasure.

It's crucial to pinpoint that emotions tied to sexual experiences aren't always limited to happy or ecstatic ones. They can toggle across an entire spectrum—from excitement to nervousness, from passion to anxiety. After your first sexual experience, you might feel an unexpected mix of emotions, from joy and satisfaction to confusion or even regret. These feelings are all part of the sexual landscape, and understanding them can help demystify the emotional rollercoaster that often accompanies sexual experiences.

Emotionally preparing for sex is as important as the physical preparedness. You might question, "am I ready?" The answer is personal and varies from one person to another. Having sex shouldn't be about peer pressure or proving yourself. It should be a consensual decision made when you feel emotionally prepared and comfortable, armed with the necessary knowledge about safe sex and committed to open, honest communication with your partner.

Understanding the vital role emotions play in sexual experiences also underscores the importance of aftercare, the emotional and physical attention given to each other after sex. It could be gentle words, cuddles, or even an honest conversation. Aftercare is about ensuring emotional well-being and underlines mutual respect and care, creating space for debriefing and reassuring each other about the shared experience.

Realize that emotions around sexual experiences might change over time. The feelings you tie with sex during your teen years might evolve with age and experience, and that's perfectly okay. Emotional growth and changes in viewpoints are standard aspects of maturing.

Lastly, remember, everyone's story is unique. There's no right age, place, or way to have a sexual experience. The 'right' is what feels right for you, in line with your emotional readiness and personal values and always consistent with the principles of consent and respect. So, listen to your heart, respect your emotions, foster connections, and always ensure a safe, consensual space, because, at the very heart of a sexual experience, it's emotions and connections that truly define it.

DEMYSTIFYING SEX: SEPARATING MYTHS FROM TRUTH

Sex, a three-letter word that draws a flurry of reactions, curiosity, and unfortunately, significantly more myths than truths. As our society tiptoes around comprehensive sex education, misinformation often fills the gaps. Inaccurate ideas or misconceptions about sex can lead to confusion, apprehension, and even potential risks. Let's undertake the mission of demystifying sex, separating myths from realities and creating a safer, well-informed pathway into this aspect of our intimate lives.

First, you might have heard, "Everyone in high school is having sex." This one-size-fits-all narrative is misleading. Everyone's timeline for becoming sexually active is unique, and many adolescents actually decide not to have sex during their high school years. This decision, like the decision to have sex, should be respected as it's a personal matter dependent on an individual's emotional readiness, values, and comfort level.

Second, "The first time always hurts" is a common, yet incorrect assumption. If there's pain during intercourse, it can often be tied to nervousness, lack of effective communication, inadequate foreplay, or medical conditions. Good communication about what feels good or doesn't, ensuring consent, and taking the time for ample foreplay can ensure a comfortable and enjoyable experience.

Simultaneously, the myth of "You can't get pregnant if it's your first time having sex" needs busting. The reality is, if someone with a uterus has started their periods, they can conceive, regardless if it's the first or hundredth time engaging in sexual intercourse. Using contraceptives is necessary every time to prevent unwanted pregnancies and protect against sexually transmitted infections (STIs).

Speaking of contraceptives, the misconception that "The 'pull-out method' is foolproof" is unfortunately prevalent. The truth is, precum or pre-ejaculate can contain sperm, and the 'pull-out method' does not protect against STIs. To prevent unintended pregnancies and STIs, use reliable contraception methods like condoms and hormonal birth control and only rely on advice from trusted health sources.

"You can't get an STI from oral or anal sex," is another dangerous myth. The truth is, most STIs can be transmitted through any sexual activity involving genital, oral, or anal contact. It's always essential to use protection during any sexual activity, including oral and anal sex.

Another must-address myth is that "If they love me, they'd have sex with me." Coercion or emotional manipulation has no place in a respectful and healthy sexual relationship. Sex should always be a mutual decision. Emotional readiness, personal values, and comfort should guide one's choice about when and with whom to engage in sexual activities. Respect and consent should be the reigning principles in your journey of sexual exploration.

Lastly, let's dispel the myth that "Sex is the ultimate demonstration of love or commitment." Intimacy can be shared and expressed in countless ways apart from sex—through shared experiences, meaningful conversation, or simply spending time together. Love and commitment aren't solely proven through sexual activity.

The world of sexual education is, unfortunately, a maze teeming with misinformation. However, by actively dispelling these myths and painting a clear, factual picture, we can navigate this territory confidently and safely. After all, knowledge carries the power to transform our experiences, imbuing them with safety, respect, and enjoyment. So let's commit to prioritizing accurate information, dispelling myths, and paving the path for a healthier, happier understanding of our sexual lives.

ANTICIPATING THE FIRST TIME: HOPES AND REALITIES

The 'first time'—an aspect of becoming that sparks innumerable fantasies, questions, and occasionally, fears. The anticipation of your first sexual encounter can stir a whirlpool of emotions. One minute, it's woven with blushes and butterflies; in the next, it might feel like a strange, riddled territory inciting nerves. It's important to realize that these emotions are entirely normal and surprisingly universal among teens approaching the threshold of their sexual lives.

Hopes tied to the first sexual experience often orbit around ideals absorbed through media, conversations, or surrounding societal narratives. You might envision it as a seamless, near-magical episode, happening under perfect circumstances, with the 'perfect' person, wrapped in passionate romance, and delivering an explosion of pleasure. While this could be reality for some, it's essential to peel back the layers of these expectations and align your anticipation with reality.

The reality of one's first-time anchors itself in variations more than in absolities. It's different for everyone, steeped in personal truths rather than universal laws. The 'perfect' situation is highly subjective, dependent on personal comforts, readiness, and consensual agreement with your partner. It may not be a fireworks display of intense pleasure but a delicate exploration of newfound intimacy. It's seldom perfect—in fact, it can be awkward and sometimes, not as pleasurable as expected. However, these realities should not breed disappointment or regret.

No two first sexual encounters are the same. Some might be filled with mutual affection and understanding, while others might echo with apprehension and anxiety. Some may lead to immediate bonding while others might need more time to kindle a deeper connection. The key lies in realizing that your first time doesn't set in stone the course of your sexual future—it's merely the starting point of a long, personal journey of discovery.

Prepare, both physically and emotionally, before embarking on your sexual journey. Talk openly with your partner about your anxieties, expectations and boundaries. Always consent enthusiastically, and ensure your partner does, too. Get familiar with contraceptive methods and their proper usage. Understand the importance of sexual health and regular check-ups. Arming yourself with the right information and tools can drastically reduce feelings of fear or uncertainty, paving the way for a safe, healthy, and fulfilling experience.

Understand that practicing intimacy runs deeper than the act itself— it's about fostering a connection, nurturing trust, and navigating vulnerability. Emotional harmony with your partner, open communication, and mutual respect contribute significantly more to your experience than mere physicality.

Refrain from measuring your experience against media portrayals or peers' narratives—this journey is about you and your partner exclusively. Don't rush into it pressurized by societal norms or friends. Wait until you're fully ready and comfortable.

It's okay if your first time veers off the commonly-told script—it's okay if it's not shrouded in rose-tinted perfection. It won't necessarily define your sexual experiences thereafter. It's not a test you pass or fail—it's a step you take when you're ready, with someone you trust.

As we anticipate our first sexual experience within the kaleidoscope of hopes and realities, remember that it's in our hands to navigate this journey with respect, understanding, and patience. Equip yourself with knowledge, communicate, consent, and most importantly, be kind to yourself during this exploration. Here's to your journey into the realms of intimacy—May it be safe, mutual, and a stepping stone towards understanding and embracing your sexual self.

SEX IN THE SOCIAL CONTEXT: NAVIGATING CULTURAL NORMS

As we continue exploring intimacy and sex, it becomes clear these experiences do not exist in a personal vacuum—they occur within a wider social context. The values and norms held by our culture, community, and family often determine our attitudes towards sex. The lens of social context meaningful shapes our understanding and expectations of sexual experiences.

Depending on the cultural environment, our conversations, beliefs, and attitudes about sex vary greatly. Some communities might be more open about discussing sex, facilitating more informed and empowered adolescents. Conversely, societies where sex is a taboo might inspire an atmosphere of secrecy and misinformation—an environment that breeds potentially harmful myths and stereotypes.

With increasing digital connectivity, cultural norms are becoming more varied and complex. The rapid influx of global perspectives paves the way for broader mindsets. However, it also magnifies the risk of exposure to harmful, unrealistic expectations about sex, often exacerbated by misleading depictions of sex in mainstream media. These portrayals can skew perceptions, inciting pressure to conform to perceived 'standards' of looks, behavior or performance.

The most balanced approach is to filter these societal and cultural influences through a sieve of critical thinking. Understand what feels personal and true to you, separate from societal stereotypes or pressure. This cultivation of personal understanding is critical—only you get to decide your sexual journey and its timeline, within the parameters of mutual consent and respect.

Navigating sex within the societal context also transcends to understanding sexual rights. Understanding your right to consent, the right to sexual health information, the right to say no, and the right to enjoy healthy, safe sexual experiences, is vital. While cultural fabric can tightly shape perceptions of sex, personal rights and safety must transcend these cultural constraints.

Another critical aspect of navigating sex in the social context is respecting the varied experiences of others. The diversity of experiences, emotions, and timelines regarding sex is perfectly normal. Your journey might look entirely different from your peers, and that's okay. Foster an environment of respect, free from teasing, pressure, or judgment.

The societal context is an undetachable backdrop of our sexual lives. However, the key lies in navigating these societal and cultural norms without compromising personal comfort and readiness. Engage in dialogue, analyze your values and expectations, respect others' experiences, and stand firm in your sexual rights. By doing so, you can navigate cultural norms while carving out your unique journey towards understanding and exploring intimacy.

Remember, your journey is yours to direct, and within this social tapestry, it's okay to draw your thread. Cultural influences, societal norms, media propagation—they all contribute to our perceptions and conversations about sex, making them an enriching part of our journey, not the director of it. At the end of the day, your story will be yours and yours alone—unique, subjective, and immeasurably personal. So steer it with knowledge, grace, and an unwavering respect for yourself and others. And at each step, unfold a narrative that echoes not with societal dictates but with your truth, consideration and consent.

CHAPTER 3

CHOOSING PREVENTION

THE SPECTRUM OF CONTRACEPTION:
A COMPREHENSIVE GUIDE

Transitioning into sexual activity carries responsibility. It's about taking charge of your sexual health and making informed decisions. A pivotal part of this process is understanding contraception. Often deemed as a hush-hush topic, contraception plays a crucial role in preventing unintended pregnancies and sexually transmitted infections (STIs). Here, we unfold a comprehensive guide to the wide spectrum of contraception, aimed at providing you the knowledge to make confident and informed decisions about your sexual health.

At one end of the spectrum are barrier methods like condoms, diaphragms, cervical caps, or contraceptive sponges. These methods block the sperm from entering the uterus. Condoms hold a particular merit as they not only prevent pregnancies but also protect against STIs, a rare attribute in the contraception landscape. They are easily accessible, affordable, and come in male and female variants.

Hormonal methods form another significant part of this spectrum. These include birth control pills, patches, injections, or vaginal rings. They work by regulating hormones to prevent ovulation, and thus, fertilization. It's essential to remember, these methods do not protect against STIs, and most require a prescription.

Intrauterine devices (IUDs) and implants constitute long-acting reversible contraception. They are devices placed in the uterus or under the skin, releasing hormones or copper to prevent pregnancy. They are effective, long-lasting, and can be removed any time if pregnancy is desired.

Emergency contraception is another crucial part of the contraceptive spectrum. These are methods used to prevent pregnancy after unprotected sex or contraceptive failure. They include emergency contraception pills, often known as morning-after pills, and copper IUDs. While useful, they should not replace regular contraception methods and do not protect against STIs.

Natural methods of contraception include fertility awareness methods, which involve tracking menstrual cycles to avoid unprotected sex during fertile days. While no side effects or costs are associated, these methods require commitment, consistent monitoring, and do not protect against STIs.

Permanent methods of contraception, such as vasectomy and tubal ligation, are options for those absolutely certain they don't want future pregnancies. These procedures are effective but are typically irreversible.

Selecting contraceptive methods requires careful pondering about lifestyle, health history, frequency of sexual activity, number of partners, future pregnancy plans, and comfort level. You must have open conversations with healthcare providers or trusted adults to make an informed decision that suits your lifestyle and needs.

Understanding the spectrum of contraception equips you to take charge of your sexual health, empowering you to make informed decisions about preventing unintended pregnancies and protecting against STIs. The options are varied; what matters is the choice feels right for you. Oh, and remember, it's okay to switch methods if one isn't working out—this journey is about finding what's best for you. Here's to understanding, choice, and taking charge of your sexual health. In the end, remember prevention is the most powerful tool we have against sexual health concerns. So let's wield it with knowledge, confidence, and utmost responsibility.

MAKING INFORMED CHOICES: SELECTING CONTRACEPTIVE METHODS

Making the choice to become sexually active is significant, but choosing a suitable contraceptive method is equally important and honestly, just as personal. It's not merely a step in the preparation towards intercourse; it's an exercise in embracing responsibility and an act of respect—for yourself and your partner. As you shuffle through options, it's vital to equip yourself with the right knowledge, opening the doors to informed decision-making about contraception.

A suitable contraceptive method goes beyond popularity, comfort, or convenience. It equally hinges on lifestyle, health conditions, frequency of intercourse, the number of sexual partners, and future family planning. Being honest about your lifestyle and personal circumstances helps tailor a contraceptive plan that fits you well.

Consider the frequency of your sexual activity. If you're sexually active regularly, hormonal methods like birth control pills, patches, or vaginal rings are effective. However, these require daily or weekly administration, which calls for diligence. If you're someone who struggles with routines, long-acting reversible contraceptives, like IUDs or implants, might be more suited. If your sexual engagements are infrequent or unplanned, keeping a supply of condoms or having knowledge about emergency contraception can be beneficial.

Quickly survey your health conditions. If you're nursing certain health problems or are on specific medications, some contraceptive methods might not be suitable. For instance, some hormonal contraceptives are unsuitable for those with blood clotting disorders or certain types of cancers. A candid conversation with your health care provider can help you make a choice keeping health circumstances in consideration.

Next, contemplate protection against sexually transmitted infections (STIs). If STI protection is a priority, which it should be, especially if you have multiple partners, condoms are the way to go. They are the only contraceptives that offer STI protection. You can combine condoms with other contraceptive methods for pregnancy prevention, giving you a kind of safety combo.

Your plans for a future family might be vague or firmly etched plans in your mind. If you see children in your future, reversible methods like condoms, pills, or IUDs offer flexibility. However, if you're sure about not wanting to conceive ever, permanent methods like vasectomy or tubal ligation could be explored.

Consider side effects. Each method comes with possible side effects. Hormonal methods might trigger mood changes, weight gain, or acne in some, while others might not face any of these. IUDs might cause cramping or irregular periods initially, while condoms are usually side-effects free. An open discussion with your healthcare provider can detail potential side effects, aiding an informed choice.

A final consideration is affordability and access. Understand the cost, need for prescription or not, and insurance coverage for each option to select the most viable one.

In the end, remember there's no perfect one-size-fits-all contraceptive method. It's okay to experiment with different methods till you find the one that fits you best. Over time, as your life circumstances change, your birth control method might change too—that's completely normal. Contraception is an empowering part of your sexual health, offering control, safety, and peace of mind. It's about choosing to protect—protect against unplanned pregnancies, protect against STIs, and protect your future. So, take a deep breath, gather your facts right, and make your informed choice. After all, you're not just choosing a contraceptive method, you're choosing accountability of your sexual health, and that's a choice worth applauding for!

▮ DEBUNKING BIRTH CONTROL MYTHS

As much as we crave to take charge of our sexual health, it's common to encounter pesky myths about birth control that can skew our perspective and our choices. These myths, whispers passed from generation to generation, friends to friends, or strewn across the digital landscape, often create harmful roadblocks to appropriate sexual health education. It's time we crack these myths wide open, replacing misinformation with science-based truths.

Myth number one: "Birth control pills make you gain weight;" a commonly held belief that instills unnecessary fears. Truth be told, most users of the pill do not gain weight. It's different for different individuals, and a comprehensive study found no significant link between hormonal birth control and weight gain.

Myth two: "The pill works immediately." A faulty idea that could lead to unintended pregnancies. Reality dictates that the pill takes about seven days to become effective. In some cases, depending on when in your cycle you start, it might take a full month. Until then, utilize other forms of contraception like condoms.

Another myth making rounds: "Taking birth control for a long time will affect your fertility." Contrary to this misconception, hormonal birth control does not affect long-term fertility. It temporarily prevents pregnancy, and once discontinued, your body resumes its normal fertility levels.

A rampant myth is, "You need to take a break from hormonal birth control every couple of years." This erroneous piece of advice not only interrupts routine but also potential protection. There's no medical advantage to taking a break. In fact, continuous use of hormonal birth control can provide you with long-term benefits, including reducing the risk of ovarian and endometrial cancer.

Here's a noteworthy myth: "Birth control pills protect against STIs." Unfortunately, this isn't true. Except for condoms, no other birth control method protects against STIs. No matter what other contraception you're using, always use condoms during intercourse to provide the best protection against STIs.

A prevalent misconception is, "Emergency contraception is an abortion pill." This is fundamentally incorrect. Emergency contraception prevents pregnancy, either by delaying ovulation or preventing fertilization. It does not terminate an established pregnancy.

The final myth is an old tale: "Using two condoms provide double protection." The pure intention behind this myth might be safety, yet in reality, the friction between two condoms may increase the risk of breakage, making it less safe than using just one.

Debunking these myths is more than fact-checking—it's cleaning up the road for reliable, comprehensive sex education. It's about breaking misinformation chains and bringing scientific, factual information to the forefront. The world of contraception is diverse, filled with potential choices to fit your needs. To navigate this ecosystem effectively, debunking myths is as crucial as understanding options. Factual information empowers us to make the best decisions for our bodies, lives, and futures. It's the first step in taking control of your sexual health and ensuring safe, comfortable sexual experiences. Let's consider it our collective responsibility to debunk, to sift through the fiction, and assert the reign of facts. Because, ultimately, only through knowledge can we transform our experiences, decisions, and lives. And when it comes to sexual health – the abilities to prevent unplanned pregnancies, and safeguard future choices – knowledge is, indeed, the most empowering tool.

| NAVIGATING HEALTH AND CONTRACEPTION

Navigating one's sexual health and contraception can initially seem like traversing uncharted territory. However, armed with knowledge, these intricate maps can be deciphered with ease. When it comes to contraception, individual needs, comfort, and overall health play pivotal roles in steering the journey, making it a personal, often profound narrative of empowerment and responsibility.

Health considerations stand at the heart of effective contraception selection. Certain health conditions, both physical and mental, may influence the effectiveness and safety of some contraceptive methods. For instance, some forms of hormonal birth control might not be suitable for individuals on certain medications or those with a history of blood-clotting disorders. Similarly, physical conditions like latex allergies could influence the type of condoms used. Thus, it's imperative to initiate open conversations with your healthcare provider, discussing your medical history in its entirety.

The link between mental health and contraception also demands attention. Hormonal fluctuations induced by some contraceptive methods can affect mood and emotional well-being. If you're experiencing mental health conditions like depression or anxiety, finding a contraception method that minimally affects your emotional landscape becomes essential. This significance of this aspect often gets overshadowed, but remember—your mental well-being is as crucial as your physical health when it comes to making contraceptive choices.

Behavioral lifestyle factors like smoking, or even your body weight, can influence the safety and efficacy of certain contraceptives. For instance, smokers over 35 have higher risk factors associated with using hormonal birth control. It's therefore essential to discuss these factors openly and honestly with your healthcare provider to ensure you're making the safest choice.

Sexual health isn't limited to the physical dimension—it extends to psychological well-being, quality relationships, and responsible, satisfying sexual experiences. Prevention or detection of diseases, comprehensive sex education, access to contraception, and control over reproductive choices are fundamental aspects of sexual health. As you navigate these aspects, be proactive—regular screening for STIs, understanding the signs of healthy and unhealthy relationships, taking charge of protection—are all part of this journey.

Contraception serves as a bridging element between sexual activity and overall health—navigating this can be empowering and liberating. It enables control over reproductive choices, reduces the risk of unintended pregnancies and STDs, and affords the freedom to enjoy sexual activity responsibly and safely.

In the course of your sexual health journey, there may be confusion, apprehensions, and countless questions. Recognize that it's okay to ask, to seek help. Reach out to healthcare providers, trusted adults, or reliable online resources. This is your journey, and you have every right to comprehend every curve, every corner in your course fully.

Remember, when it comes to sexual health and contraception—knowledge, honesty, and proactive involvement are your guiding stars. This path, though personal and unique for everyone, should always be anchored in respect—respect for your well-being, respect for your partner, and most vitally, respect for informed decisions. Here's to you, steering your journey, navigating health and contraception, and positively shaping your present and future. Explore, ask, learn, and evolve. Because your sexual health narrative doesn't just contribute a chapter in your life—it forms a pivotal plot, with you holding the authorial power. Own it.

| THE SAFETY NET: UNDERSTANDING EMERGENCY OPTIONS

Navigating prevention in sexual health often prompts us to build reliable safety systems. These systems ideally entail regular contraception use, routine health check-ups and the adoption of healthy sexual behaviours. Yet, things don't always go as planned—contraceptives might fail, or lapses could occur in judgement or preparation. Having a safety net for such instances becomes paramount. This safety net materializes in the form of emergency contraception options—an essential part of your sexual health toolkit.

Emergency contraception is essentially a means to prevent pregnancy after unprotected sex or in case a contraceptive method fails—for instance, a condom breaks or a birth control pill is missed.

It offers a second chance to prevent pregnancy, acting like a safety net preventing you from landing into an unintended pregnancy.

Two primary types of emergency contraception exist—emergency contraception pills (ECPs) and Copper intrauterine devices (IUDs). ECPs, often known as "morning-after pills", work by delaying or inhibiting ovulation, hence preventing fertilization. There are two kinds: one contains ulipristal acetate, prescribed by a healthcare provider, and the other contains levonorgestrel, available over-the-counter without age restrictions. It's crucial to take these pills as soon as possible within 72 hours after unprotected sex—the sooner, the better.

An alternative emergency contraception method is the Copper IUD— a small device inserted into the uterus by a healthcare provider within five days of unprotected sex. The Copper IUD primarily prevents the sperm from reaching and fertilizing the egg. It is the most effective form of emergency contraception available and has the added advantage of providing long-term contraception if you choose.

While emergency contraception presents an invaluable option in specific scenarios, it's important to understand its limitations and nuances. First, they are not intended as regular birth control—these are for emergencies and should not replace regular contraceptive methods. Second, the efficacy wanes as time passes after the incident of unprotected sex. Third, an essential point to note— emergency contraception does not protect against sexually transmitted infections.

While offering you a much-needed safety net, emergency contraception is not an excuse to ignore regular contraception. It's like an airbag in your car—it's there if you need it, but it doesn't mean you can skip wearing your seatbelt.

The essence of understanding emergency contraception options embodies the larger realm of sexual responsibility—informed choices, prevention, and safety. Use technology, digital platforms, speak to healthcare professionals, and educate yourself. Knowing your options ensures control over your sexual health and choices, enabling proactive measures rather than reactive steps.

Being equipped with the right knowledge, including the understanding of emergency contraception, promotes sexual empowerment—a power married with responsibility and respect. So, as you delve deeper into your journey of understanding, exploring and living your sexual health, let knowledge be your constant ally and guide. Every stitch of information, every brokered myth adds a layer of strength to your safety net, making it more robust, dependable—a guarantee that sexual health isn't just a segment of your life but forms a core fiber of your overall health and happiness. With this understanding, tread with confidence, coming one step closer to fostering a healthier, informed, and empowered you.

CHAPTER 4
STIS UNCOVERED

STIS DEMYSTIFIED: KNOWLEDGE IS POWER

Embarking on the journey of sexual health and exploration, amidst its enriching experiences and complex emotions, comes the responsibility of understanding sexually transmitted infections, or STIs. Often shrouded in myths, stigma, and misinformation, STIs are realities that need to be openly demystified and discussed. As the adage goes, knowledge is power, and this power is a critical keystone in the viaduct towards sexual health.

Defining STIs (sexually transmitted infections), sometimes referred to as STDs (Sexually Transmitted Diseases), is the first step in gaining understanding. STIs are infections that pass from person to person during sexual intercourse or intimate contact. They can affect anyone, regardless of age, gender, or sexual orientation. The most commonly known STIs include chlamydia, gonorrhea, genital herpes, HIV/AIDS, HPV, syphilis, and trichomoniasis.

It's vital to remember that STIs can often be silent spectators in your body, not causing noticeable symptoms immediately, or even at all—which is why regular testing becomes crucial. However, when symptoms do appear, they can range widely based on the specific infection - from discomfort during intercourse, abnormal discharge, to more severe symptoms like pelvic pain or even flu-like symptoms.

A common myth about STIs is that they can only spread through penetrative sex. The reality is, STIs can spread through all kinds of sexual contact—vaginal, oral, and anal—and in some cases, even through intimate skin-to-skin contact.

Another prevalent misconception is, "If you and your partner don't show symptoms, you're not at risk." A deceptive myth, considering many STIs can be asymptomatic, meaning the person carrying the infection won't display any symptoms, but can still pass the infection to their partner.

Demystifying STIs involves understanding the plausibility of multiple STIs. Contracting one STI doesn't make you immune to others, nor does it prevent you from getting infected with the same STI again in the future. Additionally, having an STI can increase your chances of contracting another, making prevention efforts even more critical.

Perhaps, the most significant myth surrounding STIs is the stigma. STIs are a purely medical condition, and not a moral verdict—they are not an embarrassment or a character flaw, and individuals with STIs are not 'dirty' or 'promiscuous.' It's time we split STIs from these destructive beliefs and treat them like what they are—health issues requiring attention, understanding, and care.

It is crucial to arm ourselves with the understanding that though STIs can be uncomfortable and frightening, most can be cured, and all can be managed with the right treatment. This underscores the importance of regular testing, early detection, and prompt treatment procedures.

Unlocking the truths about STIs is empowering—not only does it equip individuals with the power to protect themselves and their partners, but it also helps combat the shame and silence surrounding STIs. The realm of deeply personal, often daunting narratives of sexual health, requires knowledge as a beacon, shedding light on the misconstrued, the stigmatized facets like STIs. It's through this collective illumination that we can build the solidarity of understanding, lay the groundwork for meaningful conversations, and weave a tapestry of responsible sexual culture— a culture that honors transparency, embraces precautions, and above all, values health. Knowledge about STIs isn't just power—it's your shield, your guide, and your stepping stone toward an aware, informed, and healthier future, a promise towards a better you. Therefore, continue to ask, learn, share, and above all, stay proactive about your sexual health—for that is the hallmark of sexual empowerment.

STRATEGIES FOR PREVENTION AND PROTECTION

Preventing sexually transmitted infections (STIs) might seem like navigating a minefield, particularly when embarking on sexual exploration. Yet, incorporating specific strategies and measures into your sexual conduct can significantly reduce the risk, transforming apprehension into empowerment and effectively taking control of your sexual health.

Foremost, understand the power of protection. Among various methods, notably, condoms rule supreme when it comes to preventing STIs. Using a condom every time you indulge in sexual activity—be it oral, vaginal, or anal—offers a robust layer of defense against infections. Female condoms too provide a good barrier against STIs. However, phrased carefully here—condoms reduce the risk, they don't guarantee 100% protection. Even then, it's the single most crucial step towards STI prevention.

Next, consider the rule of testing. Regular STI testing is a cornerstone of preventive efforts that's often overlooked due to myths, embarrassment, or generally, the lack of awareness. An STI can be a silent lurker in your body, showing no symptoms but still transmittable. Regular testing ensures early detection and timely treatment.

Vaccination is another key strategy. Safe and effective vaccines exist for hepatitis B and HPV (Human Papillomavirus). These vaccines represent significant discoveries in preventing STIs, and availing them can act as a game-changer in your prevention plan.

A worthwhile strategy to reduce the risk of STIs involves maintaining a long-term mutually monogamous relationship with a partner who has been tested and is known to be uninfected. While it might seem challenging at first, consistent communication and trust can smooth the path to this commitment.

Being knowledgeable about your partner's sexual health might be awkward but is essentially crucial. Building an open conversation about STIs, former partners, and testing history before becoming intimate can safeguard the health of both partners involved.

Moderating alcohol and drug use can also assist in preventing STIs. In a state of impaired judgement, access to sense and prevention often dwindles, leading to increased risks. Being mindful of consumption, therefore, can be a rewarding preventive measure.

Combining these strategies through consistent practice can materialize into a powerful shield against STIs. It's essential to understand that these strategies are tools, and their effectiveness boils down to truthful implementation. It might be difficult; some measures might seem too daunting while some might appear unnecessary. Yet, each cautious step, each preventive act, is a stride towards ensuring your sexual health and overall well-being.

At the intersection where understanding STIs and implementing these strategies meet resides empowerment—the ability to control your sexual health narrative actively. It's about proactive decisions, responsible choices, and respect for your and others' health.

Nonetheless, the utmost strategy is to embody an attitude of no-judgement. Confronting STIs without shame or embarrassment, seeking help, ensuring necessary measures—they demand affirming and practicing acceptance. Engage in conversations, challenge the stigma, ask for help, take control—because as much as STIs are an aspect of sexual engagements, so is prevention your right. Owning your sexual narrative and ensuring its safety forms the essence of sexual maturity—a maturity enhanced by awareness, shaped with respect, and wielded with responsibility.

So, as we unravel this realm—prevention and protection against STIs—we add layers of strength to your defense against these infections. Each strategy contributes a piece towards creating a complete puzzle of protection, enabling you to employ these strategies not only as measures but as affirmations of your commitment towards your health—a commitment forging the way for a healthier, informed, and safer future.

| RECOGNIZING SIGNS AND SEEKING TREATMENT

Recognizing the signs and symptoms of sexually transmitted infections (STIs) forms a key fulcrum in your sexual health management strategy. It bridges the gap between suspicion and confirmation, uncertainty and action. But it's also essential to remember that many STIs don't produce obvious symptoms, making regular testing critical.

Still, awareness about potential symptoms can guide us during periods of concern or doubt. Physical discomfort, unusual discharge, or visible anomalies in genital areas could be indicative of an STI. Symptoms may include burning sensation during urination; discomfort during sex; abnormal bleeding, especially after intercourse; itchy or irritated genital areas; sores, bumps, or rashes in the genital area, mouth, or anus. For some STIs, flu-like symptoms, including fever, body aches, and swollen glands, might be the first to manifest.

It's important to remember that symptoms—if they occur—may present themselves differently depending on the type of STI. For instance, the presence of painful sores might indicate herpes, while an unusual discharge or burning during urination might point toward chlamydia or gonorrhea. Human Papillomavirus (HPV) might cause genital warts, whereas other types of HPV can lead to certain types of cancers. Hepatitis, which is often sexually transmitted, might bring about flu-like symptoms, along with jaundice-like manifestations.

If you suspect that you have an STI or have had sex with someone who might have an STI, the next crucial step is seeking help and treatment. It's natural for many to feel anxious or embarrassed at this juncture, but remember—sexual health is a vital aspect of your overall health, caring for it is not just important, it's necessary.

Immediately consult a healthcare professional if you observe potential signs of an STI or have reasons to believe you may have been exposed to one. Openness and honesty about your symptoms, sexual history, and concerns are foundational to accurate diagnosis and effective treatment.

Upon suspecting an STI, some steps you can take include abstaining from sexual contact until you've consulted with a healthcare professional; scheduling an appointment with your doctor or a sexual health clinic at the earliest; and mentally preparing to discuss your symptoms, sexual history, and safe sex practices honestly.

Treatment options for STIs vary depending on the type of infection. Bacterial STIs—such as chlamydia, gonorrhea, and syphilis—are typically curable with antibiotics. For viral STIs—like herpes, HIV, and HPV—there might not be a cure, but treatments can manage symptoms, reduce outbreaks, and minimize transmission risks. Early diagnosis is often the key to more effective treatment and preventing further spread.

Navigating the aftermath of an STI diagnosis might induce feelings of anxiety, shame, or fear. But remember—experiencing an STI is not a verdict on your character or future; it's a health condition requiring attention and care. Lean on support systems—reach out to a trusted friend or find a counselor or support group. Take care of your mental health alongside your physical well-being.

In the journey of STI recognition and treatment seeking, the destination is not only about mitigating an immediate concern but about gaining knowledge, experience, and a healthier perspective towards sexual health. Consider this journey as a part of your growing wisdom—a lesson that teaches empathy, self-care, and above all, the capacity to seek help when needed. Believe in the power of recognizing the signs and seeking treatment, because these steps lead not just to recovery but also to a renewed understanding of your body and well-being—a raw, empowering narrative of resilience and respect.

THE STI CONVERSATION: HEALTH AND RELATIONSHIP IMPACTS

In the roadmap of sex education, the STI conversation isn't a mere pit stop. It's a path of its own—a dialogue that influences both personal health and relationship dynamics. Holding its own against silence, stigma, and hushed whispers, this dialogue demands honesty, courage, and empathy from everyone involved.

The health impacts of STIs are multifold. If left untreated, some STIs might lead to severe health conditions. For instance, untreated chlamydia and gonorrhea can cause pelvic inflammatory disease in females, potentially leading to infertility. HPV can cause cervical and other cancers, while untreated syphilis can impact the brain and other organs. HIV, if left untreated, can develop into AIDS and critically affect the immune system. It's important to note here—the sooner an STI is diagnosed and treated, the fewer the health complications.

But the conversation doesn't end at discussing health impacts. STIs can also impact relationships—creating tension, causing distress, or even triggering the fear of disclosure. The prospect of having to inform a partner about an STI can be daunting. Fear of reaction, stigma, and the potential for relationship impact might create reluctance. Yet, it's an essential conversation to have.

When disclosure feels overwhelming, remember that it's a mark of respect and honesty towards your partner. You allow them the right to make informed decisions about their health and intimacy. Sure, the conversation might be difficult but pushing past the awkwardness is part of the responsibility that comes within the spectrum of sexual activity. Approach the conversation in a straightforward, non-panicked manner—share what you know, how you're planning to handle the situation, and what preventive or care measures need taken.

Besides disclosing to partners, the STI conversation extends to healthcare professionals, too. Its importance is undeniable, as is the potential discomfort. But remember—medical professionals are bound by confidentiality, and their main concern is your well-being. Being candid with them only helps in receiving the best possible care.

An STI can impact self-esteem and mental health. Feelings of shame, self-blame, or stigmatization are potent reactions, but they need confrontation. Reach out to trusted friends, join support groups, seek professional help if needed. Affirm that having an STI does not denote failure or moral lapse. It's part of a health condition, and it doesn't define you.

The STI Conversation is a two-way street. While it encompasses talking about your STIs or symptoms, it equally emphasizes asking about your potential partner's STI status. Like trusting someone with your STI status, trusting them with the question turns the table but is equally crucial in forging a healthy sexual relationship.

The STI conversation is as much about the self as it is about the other person involved - understanding your recovery or treatment process, reinventing sexual health measures, and acknowledging the potential impact on mental well-being.

In handling the STI conversation—whether disclosure or query—approach it as a narrative of respect—respect for one's health and the health of others. It takes bravery to engage in difficult conversations, and this bravery deserves recognition and commendation. By speaking up, by seeking advice, and by prioritizing health, you contribute to a broader dialogue—one that gradually shuns stigma and shines a light on the importance of transparency, thereby fostering an environment rich in trust, understanding, and wellness. This isn't just a conversation for the present moment—it's a dialogue for healthier futures, stronger relationships, and empowered individuals who assert control over their well-being. Embrace this conversation, for it does not weaken; it empowers and uplifts. It's your voice in the vast echo chamber of sexual health, and it matters deeply. Remember, your voice is powerful, and in these echoes, it finds resonance and strength—an undying melody of resilience and courage.

| THE IMPORTANCE OF BEING TESTED

When it comes to managing your sexual health, regular testing for sexually transmitted infections (STIs) becomes as fundamental as the very precautions taken to avoid them. It surfaces as a crucial pillar, holding up the fortress of sexual well-being. However, the significance of STI testing often gets overshadowed by misconceptions, embarrassment, or the dreaded "It won't happen to me" syndrome. It's time we see STI testing not as a sweeping wave of panic but as a lighthouse guiding us towards safer shores.

Regular STI testing is the cornerstone of prevention, early intervention, and treatment. Despite our best efforts, STIs can sometimes slip past our protective barriers. Certain STIs can be asymptomatic, meaning they present no noticeable symptoms, making one feel secure in a false sense of safety. But behind the ease, the infection can weather away a person's health, sometimes leading to severe complications like infertility, certain types of cancer, neurological issues, or the weakening of the immune system. That's where routine testing comes in—it clears the masks from silent STIs, enabling early detection, treatment, and preventing further spread.

If you're sexually active, especially if you have multiple partners or do not consistently use barrier methods like condoms, regular testing becomes a non-negotiable part of maintaining your health. It's not a one-time event; it's a crucial part of your health routine.

Scenarios like having unprotected sex, discovering that a partner has an STI, symptoms appearing, or simply, entering a new sexual relationship, call for immediate testing. However, it's crucial to make testing a priority even without these triggers.

There's a common misconception that if you 'appear' healthy or if your partner looks 'clean,' you don't need testing. STIs don't always show symptoms, and they certainly don't have a 'look.' This misplaced belief could result in undiagnosed and untreated STIs, which might later manifest into severe health complications.

Done correctly, an STI test is quick, simple, and generally painless. Depending on the STIs you're being tested for, the test may involve a urine sample, a blood sample, a swab, or a physical examination. Remember: any temporary discomfort is worth the peace of mind that comes from knowing your status.

The notion of STI testing often cohabits with fear—fear of results, fear of judgment, fear of the process itself. It's okay to be nervous, but the process is generally straightforward and supported by healthcare professionals who are there to help.

Moreover, it's crucial to remember that an STI test, regardless of the result, is not a measure of your worth or dignity. A negative test doesn't brand you 'clean,' nor does a positive one label you 'dirty.' These harmful labels uphold stigmatizing attitudes that prevent people from getting tested. An STI status doesn't define a person—it's just a part of their current health information.

If you test positive for an STI, remember—a diagnosis isn't the end of the world. It's the beginning of a treatment journey. Many STIs can be easily treated and managed, and nearly all have treatments to alleviate symptoms.

STI testing is your ally, your silent protector—one which breaks the barriers of uncertainty to clear a path of knowing and proactive responding. It's a step that reaffirms your commitment to your health and the responsibility towards your partners' health. Proactively seeking STI testing manifests as a potent act of self-care—sowing seeds of self-respect, nurturing trust within relationships, cultivating healthier communities, and ultimately—helping you seize control of your sexual narrative.

Therefore, see testing not as a mental vertigo but as a stepping stone towards improved well-being. Embrace it, advocate for it, for it holds the power to dissolve fears, alleviate worries, and spur reassurances. And in this labyrinth of sexual health, reassure yourself of your strength, resilience, and the power to take control of your well-being. Because you are more than worth it—you are every bit as deserving of this peace of mind, this clarity of your health.

CHAPTER 5
LOVE IN THE TEEN YEARS

THE LANDSCAPE OF TEENAGE RELATIONSHIPS

I n the living tapestry of human experience, teenage years embody a vibrant panorama—a melange of new emotions, a series of firsts, a journey of transformations. Love and relationships during these years, then, hold their unique hue—an alluring, yet sometimes baffling landscape that is as enriching and transformative as it is complex and challenging.

Dating and relationships in teenage years map the transition from adolescence to adulthood, acting as a rehearsal stage for future long-term relationships. A romantic relationship in your teen years can stir a whirlpool of emotions ranging from thrilling love to heartbreaking lows. The experience is underscored by the sometimes ecstatic, sometimes agonizing realization of new feelings—an exciting yet unfamiliar territory to chart.

High school halls are frequently buzzing with whispers about who's dating whom; cell phones buzz with texts of flirtation, heart emojis, and late-night chat sessions, while social media platforms see a flurry of love-laden posts, spilling the saga of teenage love. Suddenly, friends' circles may shrink or expand, interests may align or diverge, the concept of 'time' might wrap itself around someone special, and routine might find itself reshaped. Yes, teenage relationships breathe an air of constant change.

Peered through the lens of hormones and high school drama, the landscape of teenage relationships can often seem like an enclave of intense emotions, marked territories, and poignant life lessons. However, it's also, more importantly, a petri dish of personal development—an exploration of self and others that adds layers to one's understanding and perception.

Just as much as teenage relationships are about shared smiles, intertwining fingers, stolen glances, and Instagram-worthy dates, they are about self-discovery. It's during these years that many grapple with their sexuality, beginning to understand their attractions, forming a bedrock of identity. For many teens, these years could be the first time acknowledging and accepting their sexual orientation.

Dating during teenage years can also be a method of carving out individuality amidst the chaos of adolescence, nurturing personal growth. Relationships become mirrors reflecting our best and our not-so-best sides—bringing to light virtues like respect, trust, and understanding, while also pointing towards areas of growth and transformation.

However, the broad and bustling horizon of adolescence doesn't come without its shades of grey. The journey of teenage love comes speckled with challenges. Balancing academic responsibilities with relationship commitments, learning to navigate disagreements, facing the onslaught of peer pressure, and dealing with breakups can seem like an uphill battle—a battle where resilience and understanding act as indispensable companions.

Therefore, as we delve into this vibrant segment of life, remember that teenage relationships carry more than just the punch of fresh feelings, stolen kisses and shared dreams—they weave stories of exploring identities, navigating emotions, sowing seeds of respect, and above all—learning and growing. Painting these lessons into our panorama is what makes this timeline, this landscape of teenage love, an invaluable era of life—one where hearts, minds, and souls come together to orchestrate the symphony of young love.

You're not merely traversing a period; you're shaping a lifetime of growth, personal discovery, and a foundational understanding of love and relationship. Cherish it, learn from it and let it guide your transformation into adulthood. It's a ride of a lifetime with a truckload of lessons, countless beauties, and infinite possibilities. Here's to unveiling and understanding the dynamic landscape of teenage relationships.

THE HIGHS AND LOWS OF YOUNG LOVE

Young love is a thrilling rollercoaster—with its soaring highs that make hearts flutter and its gut-wrenching drops that may script tales of heartache. It's a jumble of firsts—first crush, first date, first kiss, first heartbreak—each holding its unique mix of elation and anguish.

Consider the enchanting highs—the sweetness of the initial rush, the butterflies in the stomach, the sheer excitement of someone special reciprocating your feelings, the taste of shared laughter, stolen glances and secret smiles. When an idle Tuesday suddenly mirrors the magic of a starlit Saturday only because you have plans with them or when a text containing nothing but a simple "hey" can have you grinning at your phone, it's the charm of young love at play.

Teenage love often sows the seeds of critical virtues—it nurtures empathy, fosters respect, fuels patience, and fosters the art of compromise. Amidst all their complexities, teenage relationships brew precious lessons of connection, compassion, mutual respect, and strength. This journey, bumpy yet beautiful, presents opportunities to grow as individuals and as partners.

Yet, with the euphoric highs come the inevitable lows. Heartbreak can shatter the rosy bubble of young love, leaving behind adolescent hearts to deal with the weight of disappointment, betrayal, or simply, mismatched expectations. It's almost a rite of passage—the agonizing sting of your first heartbreak, the countless nights spent overthinking, the tear-stained pillows, the fear of bumping into them at school or seeing them with someone else.

Then come the challenges of balancing love with other aspects— finding equilibrium between friends, family, academics, and a significant other is often a teetering tightrope walk. Learning to set and respect boundaries, dealing with peer pressure and jealousy, navigating intimacy, or understanding the break-up etiquette—the encounter with these lows often becomes character-defining elements of teenage years.

Equally important are the trials of external validation—how young love gets perceived by peers, family, or society can thrust extra pressure. A seemingly harmless joke about "puppy love" could undermine real emotions while family's disapproval or a friend's skepticism can cause emotional damage. Being stuck in such lows could feel isolating, but remember, it's all part of an intricate learning curve.

The whirlwind of emotions that comes with these highs and lows contributes to making us more self-aware, more in tune with what we seek from relationships, and ultimately, more prepared for the world of adult relationships. It's the whirl of these very highs and lows that cultivate resilience, understanding, and maturity.

Navigating the highs and lows, you partake in one of life's most complex dances, intertwining steps of joy, sorrow, learning, and growing. The rhythm of this dance might be overwhelming—perhaps chaotic, sometimes enchanting but understand that every step, every misstep shapes your journey—an invaluable journey of discovery, growth, self-awareness, and endurance.

As you traverse the rollercoaster path of young love, clutch on to the essence of kindness—towards yourself and towards your partner. Everyone scrambles through this maze differently and that's okay. Let these highs elevate you, let the lows inspire growth.

Embrace love's delight, brave its heartache, glean its lessons, and remember—you're not alone. The highs will uplift you while the lows will ground and prepare you for the future. Amidst it all, you continue to grow, continue to learn, and continue to shape your understanding of love. Let the highs soar, let the lows plunge because when the rollercoaster of young love rides to the finish line, your most profound triumph will be the journey itself—a journey pulsating with life, emotion, and resilience.

DISTINGUISHING HEALTHY FROM UNHEALTHY

Navigating the realm of teenage relationships comes with its batch of complexities—sometimes exhilarating, other times exhausting. In these formative years of intimate exploration, it becomes crucial to recognize the difference between healthy and unhealthy relationships. Misinterpretations might lace first relationships, painting a potentially harmful relationship as a passionate one.

Thus, understanding the distinguishing contours becomes an integral part of the teenage love journey—a knowledge that can influence present and future dynamics significantly.

Healthy relationships breathe on the pillars of respect, trust, and open communication. These are relationships where each partner feels valued, safe, and heard; where differences are approached with understanding rather than blame; where your feelings, thoughts, rights, and boundaries are respected.

A partner who supports and encourages your interests and goals, who you can laugh and be your authentic self with, crafts elements of a healthy relationship. Here, open conversation channels bloom— be it talking about how your day went or discussing your stance on key relationship aspects like sexual boundaries, privacy, and personal time. Agreement might not always be on the horizon, but there's sync in the respect and understanding of opinions.

On the other hand, unhealthy relationships are often marked by patterns of control, manipulation, and disrespect. Red flags might include consistent disregard of your boundaries, attempts at controlling your activities or your friendships, belittling comments or actions that cause hurt and embarrassment.

Situations where disagreements lead to threatening behavior, where consent gets blurred, or when you feel consistently uneasy, anxious, or fearful around them are some alarming signs of an unhealthy dynamic.

Recognize that possessiveness is not passion, jealousy is not affection, and control is not care. Love should not clip your wings but should inspire you to fly even higher. It doesn't seek to change you to fit a certain mold but embraces and respects you for who you are. An unhealthy relationship may obscure with dramatic highs and painful lows, sometimes mistaking turbulence and persistent turmoil for depth of passion. But remember, love in its true essence thrives not on chaos or control, but on mutual respect, understanding, balance, and nurturing growth.

The distinction between what feels euphoric and what feels exhausting, between a companion and a controller, between love and possession, becomes an asset that aids in creating fulfilling relationships.

However, it's crucial to remember that relationships aren't rigidly compartmentalized. Even healthy relationships can encounter periods of conflict and misunderstanding while unhealthy ones might have pleasantly comfortable moments. Relationships are complex, layered, and unique in their dynamics. What remains consistent is your right to feel respected, valued, and safe.

In discerning the shades of healthy from the hues of unhealthy, arm yourself with knowledge, interlace it with instinct, faithfulness to your self worth, and respect for your boundaries. Embrace self-awareness and courage to question and evaluate your relationships, to voice concerns, or abandon harmful situations.

In distinguishing the healthy from unhealthy, it's not just about safeguarding against relationship downfalls, but also an enriching journey towards healthier love landscapes, growing self-awareness, and a firmer grasp on your self-esteem, desires, and rights. Carry forward these insights, apply these learnings, for they sew the quilt of your growth narrative—a narrative, where you seize the reins of youthful love, steering it in the direction of respect, mutual growth, and happiness. Remember, you deserve not just love, but healthy, fulfilling love that nurtures, respects and values you, as you step into the ebb and flow of this journey.

COPING WITH RELATIONSHIP ENDINGS

Endings of teenage relationships often bear the weight of a unique sorrow—a potent blend of first heartbreak, loss, confusion, and an uncertain recovery path. It can feel like a whirlwind of powerful emotions knocking you off your balance. During these moments, it's essential to understand that it's okay to feel upset, to allow yourself to mourn the end of a relationship, and to give yourself the grace to navigate this challenging time.

The end of a relationship might bring a sudden sense of loneliness—a vacant space where shared dreams, smiles, and whispered secrets once dwelled. Nourish the vacant spot with self-love, friendships, and passions forgotten in the whirl of a relationship. Fill the silence not with rebounds or replacements but with your voice, laughter, and dreams—a solo harmony where each note sings the strength of your resilience and growth.

Temptation to hold onto what's past, to reconnect or stalk through social media, can feel overwhelming, but remember, it's okay to distance yourself. Creating space not only physically but also virtually can aid the healing process. Letting go doesn't mean banishing memories; it means choosing to focus on the present and future over a past chapter.

During this emotionally-charged phase, your feelings may bob between sadness, anger, blame, and regret. Acknowledge these feelings without surrendering to denial or guilt—these are normal responses to an emotional loss. Allow yourself to cry, to miss the 'what was,' to feel the sting of 'what could have been,' for in this acceptance lies the first step towards healing.

Break-ups also tend to strain self-esteem. During such moments, remind yourself that the end of a relationship is not a reflection of your worth. Be patient and kind to yourself—tend to your bruised heart with gentleness and understanding, acknowledging the magnitude of your courage and strength.

A valuable source of comfort and support during this time can be your friends and family. Don't wall yourself off or struggle alone—let them be your scaffolding as you navigate this rough patch. Share with them, lean onto them, and draw strength from their love and reassurance.

In the quiet aftermath of a breakup, reflecting on the relationship might offer valuable lessons. Understand what was fulfilling and what was lacking, what dynamics you adored, and what caused discomfort. However, steer clear of blame games or dissecting the 'end' inordinate times—focus on drawing insights that fuel growth, affirm self-worth, and carve a healthier relationship roadmap for the future.

Even as you strive towards recovery, remember that healing isn't a linear journey—some days, you will take huge leaps forward while on others, you might slide back into sadness or longing. It's all part of the process. Healing is not in 'moving on' but in moving forward, carrying forward the wisdom gleaned, the resilience earned, and the growth experienced.

Relationship endings can be painful, but they can also pave the way for personal growth. It forges resilience, strengthens emotional understanding, fuels self-discovery, and shapes a more refined awareness of your relationship needs and desires.

Be gentle with yourself, let time unfurl its healing touch, let the echoes of painful goodbyes transform into hopeful hellos. Because even amidst endings, you continue to grow, continue to discover, continue to shape your understanding of love. Amidst falling and picking yourself up, remember, you still blossom—a resilient, beautiful blossom thriving amidst the ebb and flow of the grand orchestra that is life. And in this blossoming, you script a narrative of courage, resilience, and unwavering strength—one where every end merely punctuates a new beginning, a new journey, a new growth. Remember, you are worthy—you are every bit deserving of love that nurtures, cherishes, and respects you.

| THE FOUNDATION OF LOVE AND RESPECT

In the realm of relationships, love and respect form an inseparable duo—a foundational cornerstone that breathes life to healthy dynamics. Love, at its core, should speak the language of respect. It's an understanding whisper echoing through your relationships, underscoring that every sentiment, every gesture, every word is etched with due regard for you and your identity.

Love that's rooted in respect empowers—it acknowledges your thoughts, emotions, and desires. It nourishes your individuality, inspires you to flourish as 'you.' Respect manifests in various forms—be it in honoring personal boundaries, listening silently when the other person talks, validating emotions, or simply, in understanding that 'no' means 'no.' It's acknowledging that a relationship comprises two individuals—each unique, each deserving of dignity and consideration.

Under the soft light of respect, love thrives—it grows beyond pretty words and into meaningful actions. It's not just about holding hands under the starlit sky; it's about holding space for vulnerability, fears, and aspirations. It's not just about celebrating the exciting highs; it's about supporting each other during the challenging lows.

Love interwoven with respect acknowledges that disagreements are not about 'winning' or 'losing.' Instead, discussions become places for understanding differing perspectives, leading to growth and strengthening the bond.

And in this harmonious dance of love and respect, maintain the rhythm of your self-respect too. Remember, a healthy relationship celebrates your worth—it doesn't diminish it. Never compromise on your dignity, your values, or your well-being for the sake of maintaining a relationship. For love devoid of respect, stripped of mutual understanding and acceptance, falls short of what love truly offers.

As you navigate this enigmatic landscape of teenage love, let respect be your compass—guiding your actions, your words, your decisions—nurturing a bond that's not just about fleeting butterflies in the stomach but one that's about shared growth, mutual understanding, and deepest respect.

As you embrace this journey, remember, love is a beautiful language—let it always conjugate with respect. Be it love for others, or the very crucial self-love, nurture it, water it with understanding, empathy, respect, and watch it bloom into a dynamic that's fulfilling, uplifting, and empowering. Because you're worthy of love, the kind of love that respects, understands, appreciates—love that truly, deeply, sees 'you.'

CHAPTER 6

THE ESSENCE OF CONSENT

The Fundamentals of Consent

At the heart of healthy relationships lies a crucial concept—consent. It's an integral element that vaults across every interaction and relationship, defining respect, boundaries, and safety. Be it the realm of friendships, romantic relationships, or sexual interactions, understanding the fundamentals of consent is paramount.

So, what does consent mean? Essentially, consent is a clear, unambiguous, and voluntary agreement to engage in a shared activity or to share personal information. It is not merely a one-time action, but a continuous process—a powerful conversation that evolves with every interaction. Consent is a shared agreement, not a medley of assumptions or mixed signals.

Consent is always informed, meaning that all parties involved comprehensively understand what they agree upon. It's not draped in hazy maybes or muffled silence—it shines in clearly communicated 'yes.' A nod of approval, sprinkling a 'yes' in a conversational flow, indicates it. And remember, consent for one thing doesn't imply consent for everything.

In teaching ourself about consent, we learn to acknowledge boundaries—our own and those set by others. We begin to respect these boundaries, to honor the line drawn, and steer free from any force that attempts to blur this line.

There's a certain authenticity that breathes in the air of consent— here, 'no' is just as powerful and valid as 'yes.' A 'no' might sweep in subtly through a discomfort in the eyes or a rigidity in the posture, or it might paint itself bold and untamed in spoken words. Regardless of how it floats into the equation, understand that a 'no' narrates a boundary, indicating a halt—a line that demands respect.

And when it comes to the dance of love and relationships, consent adorns it with respect, understanding, and communication— harnessing a space that's safe, mutually agreed upon, and mindful of individual boundaries.

Decoding the layers of consent helps craft connections that are not just about mere agreements but about shared understanding—a realization that makes relationships, conversations, and experiences richer, healthier, and safer.

As part of life's grand vocabulary, let's learn the spelling of consent, become fluent in its language, and weave it into our daily conversations. Because the realm where respect and communication color the spectrum, where 'yes' resonate in clear echoes, and 'no' finds an honored space, is where the magic happens—it's where relationships bloom into their complete, wholesome selves.

As we begin unfolding the many-folded pages of understanding consent, let's walk a path that cherishes an environment of respect, mutual understanding, and safety—celebrating not just the essence but the very fundamental of consent in carving connections that are routed in dignity, respect, and shared understanding.

▎COMMUNICATING BOUNDARIES AND AGREEMENT

In the delicate tapestry of human connections, boundaries serve as sturdy threads weaving individual spaces, respect, and safety into relationships. Amidst the myriad of these colorful threads, runs a solid line of communication tying together the fabric of mutual understanding and agreement.

Communicating boundaries is a critical life skill, especially when exploring romantic and sexual relationships. Boundaries act as personal parameters, defining what you're comfortable with, thus helping to craft relationships that respect individuality and comfort zones. This act of defining boundaries, be it emotional, physical, or digital, comes etched with self-respect, personal safety, and assurance.

Remember, it's okay, in fact necessary, to express your needs clearly—whether it's spending time alone, limiting physical affection, or keeping certain topics off conversational tables. Speaking up doesn't dilute your affection; rather, it fortifies the foundation of respect and understanding. Early and open communication of boundaries sets the stage for comfort, trust, and respect to deepen within interactions.

Equally important is the flip side of the coin—respecting the boundaries set by others, even when they might not align with your preferences. Acknowledging their comfort zones, valuing their 'no,' reflects the essence of respect and mutual understanding.

Moving on to agreements—they stand as mutual consents enriching interactions across the relationship spectrum. Communication paints authenticity into agreements—clarifying and aligning expectations, desires, and boundaries. Be it deciding what movie to watch on a date or discussing sexual intimacy, mutual agreement is the fulcrum balancing respect and shared understanding.

Clear communication also roots out ambiguity, replacing assumptions and injustices with clarity and equality. However, remember, agreement is not etched in stone—it's a fluid space accommodating changing perceptions, feelings, and comfort levels. It's an ongoing conversation, evolving with every interaction.

In this ongoing dialogue, your voice matters—your 'yes' and your 'no,' your nods and your halts, narrate your stand, your boundaries. But remember, in the vocal arena of communication, your listening skills are just as important. Hear their silence, their spoken words, their hesitations, and link these cues into your understanding.

Remember, the beauty of relationships grows not on assumptions but on open dialogues, not on force but on free will, not on invasion but on respecting individual spaces. So, speak your mind, express your boundaries, listen actively and respect what you hear.

Embark on this journey of open conversations with honesty, respect, and an understanding ear. For in the space where 'yes' and 'no' echo in clear tones, where boundaries are respected, where communication acts as the sturdy bridge connecting spaces, blossoms the essence of healthy relationships.

This dance of communication and consent, intertwined with respect, will guide you through the maze of relationships—crafting narratives that are as respectful as they are loving, as unique as they are universal.

In every interaction, assert your space, articulate your comfort, and most importantly, remember that your voice is important. Your experiences, your comfort, your boundaries, and your agreements should underpin your narrative—the narrative of a young adult navigating the world of relationships painted with respect, mutual consent, understanding, and empathy. And within these narratives, let's continue to respect and celebrate the essence of consent—one boundary, one communication, one agreement at a time.

| CONSENT ACROSS SCENARIOS

Centuries-old myths and misconceptions might try to narrow consent's essence—stretching it out only in scenarios involving physical intimacy. This limited understanding of consent risks missing out on its broader, more comprehensive implications. Consent is a universal language—it whispers in every relationship's courtyards, resonates in every interaction's echoes, painting scenarios varied and myriad.

Let's unfold consent's narrative across different scenarios. Picture a simple interaction—a friend borrowing your favorite book. Here too, consent is vital—it's the 'Yes, sure you can borrow it' that acknowledges respect for your possession.

Now, consider friendships. Here, consent arenas extend—boundary establishment, personal space, emotional comfort, and privacy. For instance, if a friend shares a sensitive issue with you and asks you not to tell anyone else, your 'yes' orients on respecting their trust and their boundaries. Love or even the closest of friendships doesn't handover an all-access pass to personal spaces or secrets—the key always lies draped with respect and permission.

Cruise on to another cornerstone of teenage life, social media—a realm where respect for consent often gets blurred. Tagging friends in a picture, sharing contact details, or posting something about someone leaves digital footprints and can have real-life consequences. Thus, seeking consent in the digital world aligns with respecting their privacy and comfort.

Now, on to the big one: romantic and sexual relationships. Consent here becomes a critical lighthouse guiding actions and decisions. Whether it's holding hands, kissing, intimate touches, or engaging in sexual activity—each step requires unwavering, clearly-communicated, enthusiastic consent. Consensual sex is about shared agreement—it's not just about saying 'no' to what you don't want, but also about actively saying 'yes' to what you do want.

Remember, consent does not wear any ambiguity—it requires a clear, verbal, and conscious agreement. It can't be assumed under any circumstances; past sexual activities don't signal 'future' consents, and the lack of 'no' doesn't mean 'yes.' Consent is a dynamic dialogue—it's a conversation that must flow unabated, seeping into every layer and level of intimacy. This respect for consent and understanding forms the founding code of the language of love—a language painted with respect, trust, and mutual comfort.

However, securing this understanding of consent across scenarios might not be a cakewalk. You might need to debunk myths, handle peer pressure, or stand against prevailing gender norms. But always remember—it's your right to establish and maintain your boundaries across every relationship, every scenario. Because at the end of the day, your comfort, safety, and respect are non-negotiable.

And as you continue to traverse these diverse landscapes, remember that the rulebook of consent celebrates autonomy—it allows you to change your mind, to pause, to stop, regardless of the scenario, regardless of the relationship.

Growing familiar with this multifaceted narrative of consent equips you to champion respect, to understand personal boundaries better, and to construct healthier relationships. It's not just about transferring the power of 'yes' and 'no', but about understanding, respecting, and celebrating this catalyst of autonomy, respect, and safety across diverse scenarios.

Developing a keen understanding of consent across scenarios and relationships becomes an essential compass—guiding you through the beautiful yet occasionally confusing journey of adolescence and into adulthood. It offers you a skill integral to human interaction—a skill that paints the world with deeper shades of respect, empathy, and understanding. Remember, consent is not an option—it's an absolute necessity, a language worth mastering, in a world that reverberates with shared respect and mutual understanding.

| HONORING REFUSAL

In the delicate algebra of human interactions, refusal often teeters on the edge of misunderstandings and invalidated emotions. Recognizing and honoring refusal—in our actions, responses, and the undertones of our conversations—becomes critically important and is a pivotal essence of the discourse around consent.

Disguised in various cloaks—a hesitant shrug, an uncomfortable silence, a whispered 'no', or a loud and clear 'I don't want to'— refusal is a boundary drawn and a testament to individual autonomy. It is the exercising of the right to disagree, to disconnect, to define one's personal limits.

Honoring refusal is not about merely stepping back—it's about understanding the importance of that 'no', acknowledging its worth, and affirming the space it carves. It's about upholding a culture that values refusal as much as it values consent.

Consider a simple sneak-peek into everyday happenings: a friend who doesn't want to lend his favorite video game, a sibling who isn't ready to talk about a problem yet, or a partner who doesn't want to engage in certain intimate activities. In all these scenarios, a 'no' is put forth—a boundary is drawn. Respecting these boundaries is what honoring refusals stands for.

Refusal can bloom on vast landscapes—it's not just about physical boundaries or spoken disagreements. It's the undisclosed emotions hanging in uneven sighs, the discomfort shifting in their gaze, the unease written subtly on their face, and other non-verbal cues silently hidden in plain sight.

While honoring a 'no' might occasionally bruise your expectations or challenge societal norms, fabulous friendships or romantic relationships aren't built on the debris of dishonored boundaries. They blossom on mutual respect—an understanding that leaves space for refusals and disagreement; they grow where 'no' is as valued as 'yes.'

The beauty of honoring refusals mingles with the art of communication—a dialogue that makes room for grievances, for concerns, for clarifications. It nudges the focus from 'why was a no said' to understanding and accepting that 'no has been said.'

This navigation through the 'no' waters does more than just affirm respect—it promotes personal growth, fostering emotional maturity, empathy, and an improved understanding of human interactions.

However, in the process of honoring others' refusals, do not forget to uphold and honor your 'no' as well. Your comfort, your boundaries, your 'no' are valid. Remember, you owe no one an apology for your boundaries—you honor them by articulating your comfort, by detonating the weight of guilt often accompanying a 'no,' allowing it to form an integral part of your personality's ebb and flow.

In every conversation, every relationship, honor the refusals—your own and those of others. Because in understanding and accepting the denial, blooms a garden of respect, a pathway of understanding, an environment that values boundaries, and a world that celebrates consent.

One refusal at a time—let's sow seeds of mutual respect and understanding, nurturing conversations that grow on the foundation of honored boundaries and respected consents. So, as we continue to navigate the winding roads of adolescence to adulthood, let's wear the badge of honor—that of valuing and respecting refusals—as a testament to growing respect, understanding, and a world that truly cherishes the essence of consent.

| UNDERSTANDING CONSENT'S LEGAL SIDE

Beyond the realm of interpersonal relationships and social implications, consent carries a legal weight that has significant consequences if disregarded or misused. While laws pertaining to consent may differ across regions or countries, the central premise stands uncompromised—it is a human right, and its violation is a punishable offense.

In the legal context, consent mainly manifests in discussions about sexual activity. Here, consent is a clear, voluntary, and informed agreement between parties to engage in sexual activity. Although laws may vary in terms of age of consent, most agree that those under the legal age cannot provide lawful consent for sexual activities. This is designed to protect younger individuals from abuse and exploitation.

There's a crucial concept in consent's legal narrative—the concept of 'enthusiastic' consent. It means that implicit in every consent for a sexual act should be enthusiasm—it cannot be coerced, manipulated, or given under influence. Silence, unconsciousness, or any form of incapacitation does not constitute consent. Additionally, prior or even current relationship status does not give automatic authorization for sexual activity—every interaction individually calls for renewed consent.

Laws are particularly stringent when no consent is obtained. Acts such as sexual assault, rape, or other forms of sexual violence pivot around instances where consent was unclear, withheld, or obtained forcibly. Any sexual activity without clear, expressed, and conscious agreement is unlawful and punishable.

Understanding the legal implications of consent helps foster a sense of personal responsibility and promotes behavior that respects others' rights and boundaries. It empowers individuals to respect others' autonomy and their decisions around personal comfort and readiness in any situation—be it posed in sexual contexts or otherwise.

Honoring the legalities of consent also means taking the initiative to educate oneself and others. Consent is about making informed decisions—it's about education, information dissemination, and constant learning. Awareness about the legal aspects of consent aids in clearing myths, wiping out misinformation, supporting informed decision-making, and promoting an environment that respects rights, autonomy, and choices.

Approaching consent with this legal understanding underscores the importance of recognizing and upholding personal boundaries and the right to autonomous decision-making both for oneself and others. And above all, it brings to fore the severe consequences that disrespecting consent entail, thus emphasizing the need for respect, mutual agreement, and understanding in all human interactions.

Remember, respect for consent isn't just about moral obligation, social courtesy, or relationship dynamics—it's also about legal responsibility. It's a thread that ties the fabric of respect, understanding, autonomy, and safety into societal norms and laws. As you continue to grow and form relationships, bear in mind these legal aspects and implications of consent—let it guide your actions, your decisions, your respect for others and their boundaries. Because you, just like everyone else, deserve to exist in a world that respects, understands, and upholds the essence of consent—be it in social corridors, romantic landscapes, friendship lanes, or in the eyes of law.

CHAPTER 7

ESTABLISHING BOUNDARIES

CRAFTING PERSONAL BOUNDARIES

In the grand theater of life, imagine yourself as the stage director with the powerful privilege of setting the stage, arranging the props, and deciding the cues. Your life, a beautiful stage where a multitude of acts unfold, deserves well-defined boundaries—your very own personal guidelines that help create balance, prioritize your emotional health, and craft relationships that respect these boundary lines.

Crafting personal boundaries is an art that's empowering. These boundaries are not ego-constructed walls aimed to isolate you; instead, they are imprints of your self-respect, markers of your individual space, and reflectors of your values. How you want to be treated, what you're comfortable with, what you consider acceptable—personal boundaries serve as the map guiding these parameters.

The first step in the process of crafting personal boundaries is developing a clear understanding of your feelings and needs. Taking this journey inward involves recognizing what makes you feel strong, safe, and positive, as well as what makes you uncomfortable or compromises your well-being.

Consider situations where you felt upset, exploited, or uneasy—those moments often signal crossing of invisible lines—lines that outline your personal boundaries. Reflect on these instances. Was it a friend casually borrowing your things without asking? Was it someone pressurizing you for personal information? Or perhaps it was a partner who assumed they could decide everything for you? Recognizing these 'crossing-the-line' moments offer starting points for defining boundaries.

Once you have a clearer understanding of your comfort zones, articulate these in clear, assertive language. Saying 'no' doesn't brand you as selfish or rude—it only shows that you value yourself, and that you stand firm on your emotional land.

Remember, this boundary crafting stage isn't a one-time labyrinth that you navigate then exit—it's an ever-evolving maze, expanding and shifting with life experiences, with growing self-awareness and understanding. What feels okay today might not be the same a few years, or even a few moments down the line— allow yourself this room to grow, to change, and to redefine your boundaries.

However, remember to be fair—not just to yourself, but to others too. Boundary setting isn't about dictating terms to make the world dance to your tunes; it's about crafting a harmonious melody where your individual notes flow synced with the symphony around you.

Establishing personal boundaries also involves respectful acknowledgment of others' boundaries—a balanced equation where you expect to be honored and in return honor their unique comfort zones.

As you navigate your teenage years, a time of self-discovery, growth, and exploration, personal boundary crafting contributes significantly to your mental and emotional well-being. Establishing clear boundaries nurtures a sense of self worth, instills a healthier understanding of mutual respect, and strengthens interpersonal relationships.

Boundaries do not argue the absence of trust, love or friendship. On the contrary, they celebrate self-love, they foster mutual respect, and they nurture healthy relationships—ones that base themselves on clear communication, heartfelt understanding, and well-respected comfort zones.

So, embark on this journey of crafting your personal boundaries— ones that honor your space, your feelings, your values. For in this space, you define the rules—you choose the kind of energy you want to invite, the interactions you wish to engage in, the people you wish to love. By crafting your personal boundaries, you're asserting your identity, tuning in harmony with your values, and giving the world around you the respectful map they need to recognize, understand, and appreciate 'you.'

| BOUNDARY TYPES AND THEIR IMPORTANCE

Personal boundaries span across a range, each carving a unique space and imprinting a distinct identity of its sphere. Consciously defining different boundary types aids in fostering a well-rounded respect for these spaces, allowing you to navigate diverse relationships and scenarios more effectively.

Physical boundaries draw the lines around your personal space and privacy, dictating your comfort with touch, proximity, and personal belongings. These are often the most visible types of boundaries, reflected in body language and personal interactions. It could mean needing more personal space or wanting to avoid certain types of physical contact. Discomfort when someone borrows your things without asking or stands too close might signal a crossing of physical boundaries. Honoring these boundaries encourages a respectful recognition of individual space and comfort.

Emotional boundaries deal with your feelings, your emotional energy, and your personal capacity to handle others' emotions. It's the self-protective barrier between you and the emotional world around you, fostering emotional health and stability. An crucial to emotional boundaries is understanding that you are not responsible for others' feelings and reactions, just as they aren't for yours. Relying on someone else for your happiness or blaming yourself for others' unhappiness might indicate blurred emotional boundaries.

Intellectual boundaries are about respecting individual perspectives, ideas, and thoughts. It's the 'agree to disagree' space, where differing opinions can exist without causing personal offense or societal discord. Healthy intellectual boundaries are reflected in open conversations, where dissenting opinions aren't suppressed, but instead valued in fostering a broader understanding.

Time boundaries encompass your precious moments, hours, and days—protecting your time from being exploited or misused. It relates closely with self-care and personal priorities, letting you preserve time for what you value most—involving activities that foster your growth or happiness. Struggling to say no to demands on your time or feeling constantly overwhelmed might hint at blurred time boundaries.

Digital boundaries are becoming increasingly important in the contemporary age—a space that often blurs the line between private and public. These involve navigating your relationships and interactions online, including who you interact with, what information you share, and how you protect your online presence. Sharing your whereabouts or personal information without your consent might suggest a violation of digital boundaries.

Recognizing these broad categories and their subtleties allows you to craft specific boundaries in each sphere, fostering a comprehensive framework for personal respect, well-being, and interpersonal dynamics. These boundary types cater to diverse aspects of your life, helping maintain a well-rounded balance of respect, autonomy, and personal safety.

The importance of these boundaries cannot be overstated—it is they that define the foundational structure of autonomy, self-respect, and personal comfort. They act as shields against exploitation—protecting your physical space, your emotions, your ideas, your time, and your digital presence. Above all, they play an instrumental role in shaping healthy relationships—ones that are marked by mutual respect, understanding, and empathy.

Let these boundaries be your map and compass—guiding interactions, relating, respects, and self-care as you navigate through the world. By honoring the unique nature of various boundaries, you not only honor your personal spaces and feelings but also cultivate an environment for others to do the same.

As we delve deeper into understanding and establishing boundaries across spheres, let's reminisce that it's about crafting spaces that respect and value your identity, your feelings, and your comfort. So, brew a harmonious blend of these boundaries, honoring each one in its unique essence, and enjoy a world that respects, understands, and appreciates 'you.'

| ADDRESSING BOUNDARY CROSSINGS

In the fluid arenas of life, despite our best intentions, boundaries sometimes blur, cross or are outrightly violated. These crossings can trigger a potpourri of emotions—confusion, discomfort, anger, or even guilt. In such instances, recognizing the crossings, and addressing them effectively ushers an essential trajectory to boundary setting.

Acknowledging the crossing is your first lever. Recognize when a boundary has been crossed—when your personal space is invaded or your deliberate no is ignored; when emotional burdens become overbearing or a digital interaction threatens your online safety. Realizing the violation lays the foundation for addressing it.

This realization often spots itself in discomfort—if you feel uneasy, pressurized, or emotionally drained, it might be because a boundary, invisible yet vital, might have been crossed. Recognizing this is a primal step towards reclaiming your space and respect.

Next, communicate—express the discomfort caused by the boundary crossing. Addressing boundary violation is not a blame-game session but a moment for transparent conversation. Use assertive communication, mirror words that value your boundaries and highlight respect towards others. A simple, 'I am uncomfortable with...', or 'I would appreciate if...' can open the gateways for an empathetic dialogue to address crossed boundaries.

It can be intimidating, yes. Emotions might dangle between guilt and anxiety but remember, your boundaries are valid, and so is your discomfort when they are crossed. You have every right to protect your space and to have your feelings respected. Communication here needs a clear, assertive, yet respectful language—a mix that maintains a balance between addressing the violation while preserving relationship sanctity.

In the conversation's realm, ensure to offer clear cues about what you find acceptable and what you don't. Precise, transparent descriptions aid in letting others understand your boundary parameters, thereby reducing future instances of crossing them.

There will be instances where addressing boundary crossings would require assistance, especially when the crossing transcends into the area of exploitation or abuse. In such scenarios, do not hesitate to seek professional help or confide in trustworthy acquaintances.

Addressing boundary crossings isn't a one-time event—it's an ongoing process and is about continual negotiation. Along this journey, equip patience and empathy as staunch companions—helping you understand unintentional crossings, deliberate violations, and all the shades in between.

Practice resilient self-care during this process. Voicing discomfort, facing confrontations, and handling guilt can be exhausting. Remember to treat yourself with kindness—breathing in self-care and dedicating time to recharge your emotional and mental space.

Crossing of boundaries does not indicate the demolition of relationships, it's an opportunity to re-establish better, healthier, and respectful ties. Each crossing is a stepping stone—a potential chance to affirm your boundaries, to raise your self-esteem, to foster stronger, more respectful relationships.

As adolescents navigating the labyrinth of personal growth, addressing boundary crossings fosters a sense of self-worth, imparts skills to handle conflicts, and promotes healthy relationships. It's not just about managing discomfort—it's about mastering the art of maintaining personal territory in junctions of mutual respect, understanding, and trust.

Remember, your boundaries weave your safe-haven, a space that deserves respect, a trace that aims to be recognized. Resilently address the crossings, decode the discomfort, and rise above these blurred lines—marching ahead on a journey that values respect, blossoms with understanding, and charts a path that truly honors the essence of boundaries.

DIGITAL BOUNDARIES: TEXTS, POSTS, AND PRIVACY

As we journey across the boundless horizons of the digital world, we navigate through text threads, social media feeds, constant notifications, and a ceaseless surge of information. Each click, each post, each interaction scripts a passage in our online narrative. Amidst this digital landscape, establishing boundaries becomes vital—an electronic outline that shields our privacy and comfort in the cyber realm.

Digital boundaries script safety protocols into our virtual interactions, reflecting notions of proper online etiquette, privacy management, and self-care. These boundaries are not firewalls programmed to isolate you—they are thoughtful settings that protect your digital footprints, guard your online presence, and ensure your virtual interactions are shaped by respect and understanding.

Determining acceptable contact forms the nucleus of digital boundaries. This could involve designating 'quiet hours' when you would prefer not to receive messages or calls or defining which conversation topics are off-limits. Remember, starting a chat thread doesn't sign a contract obliging you to be 'always available'. Your time, your attention—even electronically—deserves respect, bears value.

Privacy settings, like sentinels, guard your digital boundaries. These options provide the option of who can view your profiles, posts or shared content, allowing you to manage and control your personal information's accessibility. Regularly reviewing these settings, especially after software updates or changing platforms, ensures that your boundaries continue to protect your digital space.

Being judicious about what you share online is another integral facet of digital boundaries. Be it a tweet fueled by a sudden surge of emotions, a tagged location announcement, or a shared picture—they carve your digital identity. Reflect on each before clicking 'share'. Ask yourself—'is it necessary?', 'would I be comfortable if this information was publicly known?' Providing a conscious pause before sharing is often the firewall that prevents potential digital boundary trespass.

Just as personal boundaries require mutual respect, digital boundaries request the same. Be respectful of others' virtual spaces—avoiding unsolicited tagging, respecting their seen-but-not-replied status, refraining from posting inappropriate comments. Essentially, 'treat others how you want to be treated' holds as true in the digital zone as it does in personal interactions.

In times where combating digital disruptions can seem like a Herculean challenge, remember to enshrine self-care into your digital routine. This could mean designating device-free zones or hours, limiting social media time or ensuring your device time doesn't encroach upon your rest or rejuvenation periods. These practices tame digital chaos, framing a healthier online culture.

Digital boundaries are not autographed to exclusivity—they are subject to change, to development, to recalibration. With evolving digital platforms, algorithms, or even life changes, your boundaries may need a tune-up—an updated version of your online outline that suits your comfort, safety, and ease.

On the grand chessboard of the digital world, every click, every post, every interaction cascades into a butterfly effect—an echo that resonates in the cyber corridors. Setting robust digital boundaries ensures that this echo resounds with respect, empathy, and understanding.

So, as you weave your way across the global village of pixels, emojis, and Wi-Fi signals—each text, each post, each share—let them reflect your digital boundaries. Boundaries that guard your privacy, respect your time, and echo your comfort. Navigate the digital world with an awareness that merges the digital with the personal—a union that fosters comfort, ensures safety, and crafts a digital presence underlined with respect, understanding, and the essence of boundaries.

| EDUCATING OTHERS ON RESPECTING YOUR SPACE

One of the pivotal pages in the boundary-setting narrative is educating others about your boundaries. Having clear outlines for your comfort, your desires, and your consent matters little if they remain a clandestine monologue—unheard, unrecognized, and unrespected by those around you. Sharing your boundary preferences, grounding them in your interactions, and fostering an environment that respects these lines is a nuanced dialogue necessary to script harmonious relationships.

Transparency is a feather that paints rich hues into this process. Openly, respectfully, and assertively defining your boundaries helps the people around you understand your comfort zones. Articulating a firm no when you're uncomfortable, or expressing your need for some alone time acknowledges your boundaries in clear terms. Such transparent conversations spread a mutual understanding, making it easier for others to respect your spaces.

Equally important as expressing your feelings is the method of doing so. Shouting a boundary out of frustration or making it a footnote in humor-poised sarcasm might fail to fully communicate its importance. Calm, respectful expressions ensure your boundary is both heard and understood.

Lead by example—respecting others' boundaries fosters a respect-for-boundaries culture. When someone shares their boundary with you, honor it, respect it, even if it's different from yours. This reciprocity nurtures a dialogue of understanding, paving a path that values individual comfort and mutual respect.

While some may value your boundaries from the word go, others might test, push, or even overstep them. In such instances, reiterate your boundary assertively, highlighting the discomfort they cause when crossed. Stern, consistent reminders often make it clear that your boundaries are neither optional nor negotiable.

Remind yourself that people aren't mind-readers—conveying your comfort zones is your responsibility. Equally essential is the understanding—the right—to reset or redefine your boundaries as you see fit. Life changes, so do our preferences, our comfort zones, and so should our boundaries.

Promoting a culture that stands by respect for personal spaces and empathy towards individual comfort, educating others about your boundaries helps sculpt relationships that are molded with understanding, respect, and empathy.

One step at a time, one conversation at a time, let's define our unique spaces, our self-respect, and our mutual admiration. Then, and only then, will we truly foster an environment that values, respects, and understands the essence of boundaries.

CHAPTER 8

DIGITAL WORLDS AND RELATIONSHIPS

THE DIGITAL INFLUENCE:
NAVIGATING ONLINE INTERACTIONS

Imagine stepping onto a global platform, where the loudening whispers of hashtags color the chatter, and any corner of the world is just a click away. Welcome to the digital world. A vast cyber expanse where interactions weave into virtual threads, embroidering the fabric of our digital lives. Navigating this realm is akin to a constantly evolving dance, where each step has the potential to leave lasting footprints—imprints that shape your digital identity.

In this interconnected sphere, online interactions carve out a landscape that burgeons with networking, learning, entertainment, and social engagement. Yet, parallelly runs a streak that propagates misinformation, harbors cyberbullying, and poses privacy risks. Defining our stride on this techno-field—an alignment that balances the boons and boundaries—is an essential component of our digital citizenship.

Online interactions, unlike face-to-face exchanges, lack the nuance of body language and tone—a challenge that strings along potential scope for misunderstandings or assumptions. Defining clear channels of communication, employing positive language, and using explicit phrases can help ease this digital dialogue.

On the social media stage, remember to play your part respectfully. Use posts, comments, and shares to promote positivity, spread awareness, and voice opinions thoughtfully. Criticism is part of the dialogue but aiming for constructive criticism fosters a healthy digital culture—one that values differing perspectives yet maintains the aesthetics of respect.

Maintaining privacy in the world where 'sharing is caring' mantra dominates can seem like walking a tightrope. Applying discernment in sharing personal information, frequently updating privacy settings, and restricting location sharing are practices that cushion your digital identity.

A significant stream of online interactions swim in the sea of online friendships and relationships. Fostering these connections requires the same pillars of trust, respect, and understanding as their offline counterparts but with an added dose of digital responsibility. Being mindful of screen-time balance, respecting online boundaries, and noting that every online interaction leaves a lasting digital footprint can craft healthy online relationships.

However, the digital world is not immune to the shadows of bullying, harassment, or abuse. Recognizing such scenarios and addressing them—whether it's blocking the person, reporting the incident, or confiding in a trusted adult can act as armor during these cyber battles.

While the digital landscape unfolds in HTML codes and CSS scripts, navigating this vast expanse isn't about conquering every platform or complying with the trending hashtags. It's about carving out an online presence that mirrors your values, fosters genuine connectivity, and respects the boundary of digital citizenship.

Navigating the online world, we learn, we connect, we evolve—all in the comfort of our screens and chairs. Yet, it's essential to remember that the person on the other side of the screen is as real as the one staring at it. Each interaction, however masked in digital codes, is still a human connection—a potential to build understanding, to spread positivity, to enrich digital and personal narratives.

In this fusion of electrons and emotions, let's navigate the digital world with empathy, respect, and understanding. Embarking on this journey, stride confidently but carefully because you're not just making digital footprints; you're paving the way for a digital culture. One that promotes understanding, spreads positivity, respects privacy, and above all, values the human behind the screen. Because in this digital world lies the reflection of our evolving societal tale—a narrative that holds us all together as we navigate the web of virtual connections.

THE DOS AND DON'TS OF ONLINE DATING

With unabridged connectivity at our fingertips, finding romance has transformed into a digital liaison, where typing hearts transcend geographical bounds, and profiles become the new first impressions. Online dating, a vivid scene in today's digital theatrics, presents a unique set of opportunities and challenges. Just as with traditional dating, there are solid dos and don'ts to keep in mind as you navigate these cyber-romance avenues.

Starting on a positive note, one significant do in the world of online dating is portraying an authentic image of yourself. The virtual realm may grant the anonymity cloak, but authenticity resonates across the screen. Honesty in your profile, from using recent pictures to being genuine about your interests and life, will garner respect and attract those with shared interests.

Another important do - take your time. Online dating is not a sprint hogging for immediate romantic gratifications; it is a marathon that requires pacing of getting to know each other. The online platform may offer a fast-forward option, but letting interactions marinate over time tends to foster healthier, more meaningful connections.

Always remember the fundamental do of online dating: prioritize your safety. Avoid oversharing personal information like address or financial details. Ensuring your dating app's location settings aren't disclosing your exact location is a safety thumb rule. Trusting your instincts when something feels off also comes as a handy shield against online predators.

Now, as we slide into the don'ts lane, don't ignore the red flags. The online facade often masks realities—a reality that sadly includes scammers, catfish, and manipulators. If something feels off—be it a discrepancy in their story or an early plea for financial aid—don't ignore these red flags.

Don't be disheartened by rejections or non-reciprocated interests. The sea of online dating is vast with a variety of fish, and not every fish would fancy the bait you throw. Keeping optimism afloat and resilience as the sail often helps navigate through the tumultuous waves of online rejections.

And last but not least, don't allow online dating to consume your life. Continuously swiping or obsessively checking the app can eventually morph into a digital black hole, sucking your time, draining you emotionally. Pacing your online dating activity and maintaining a balance with your offline life ensures a healthier dating experience.

Navigating the avenue of online dating, remember that it's okay to have standards, okay not to connect with everyone, and perfectly okay to step out if it doesn't feel right. At its core, dating—online or offline—is about forging connections that uplift your happiness quotient, resonate with mutual understanding, and honor respect.

Online dating may seem like navigating a romantic wilderness with heart-tugging allure around each corner. In this journey, arm yourself with integrity, patience, and wisdom—weapons that not just thread the path of online dating but also scribble a tapestry of enriching connections, meaningful interactions, and, quite possibly, enduring love. Remember, as the digital sun dawns on your cyber love adventure, may love's compass guide you through each text, each swipe, each heart emoji—a journey where you find not just a match in profiles but echoes in hearts.

| SOCIAL MEDIA'S ROLE IN MODERN RELATIONSHIPS

5739Hidden behind phone screens and curated posts, the palpitation of modern relationships finds an amplified echo in social media corridors. Today, hashtags not only trend digital movements but also embrace phases of contemporary romance—from the first digital introduction to shared posts etching journey milestones and sometimes, the often-dreaded 'It's complicated' status. In this digital panorama, social media paints a vibrant backdrop that colors facets of modern relationships.

For starters, the digital sphere serves as a platform for new connections. From friendship requests to shared interests, budding romances often sprout amidst these virtual threads. Whether reconnecting with a high school friend or discovering ties through a shared fandom, social media often gives love stories their initial bookmark.

As relationships bloom, social media embraces a field, scripting a narrative echo of the relationship. A space where birthday wishes adorn elaborate affection, an avenue where anniversary posts flaunt shared memories, a stage where each shared picture weaves a warp and weft into the relationship chronicle. Through likes, emojis, and comments, participants narrate their stories, while spectators become an extended part of the journey.

Revealing a relationship status, posting cozy pictures, or expressing love digitally—these are decisions each couple faces in the digital age. And with these decisions comes a spectrum of situations that need addressing. While some find comfort in public expressions of love, others might prefer the private echoes of their bond. Navigating these nuances requires open dialogue, mutual agreement, and respect for each other's comfort zones.

Yet, just like every coin, social media's role in relationships also serves a flip-side—a side shaded with misunderstandings, jealousy, and sometimes, heartbreak. The illusion of perfect relationships, constant digital availability, or public airing of private disputes can turn social media into a catalyst for relationship conflicts.

To walk this tightrope without slipping into the pitfalls, understanding each other's digital boundaries is the key. Be it about deciding when to click 'in a relationship' status or confronting issues offline before posting online—it is the quorum of mutual respect and understanding that explores social media's potential positively. The understanding that the relationship shared between two hearts transcends the digital declarations or the lack thereof sets the stage for healthy social media habits.

Acceptance plays a pivotal role in this digital dance. Accept that not everything seen on social media mirrors reality, accept that partners might have different digital comfort zones, and above all, accept that a healthy relationship blossoms beyond the digital screen's glow.

Navigating the role of social media in relationships isn't some encrypted code—it's about enhancing the positive aspects while being aware of potential falls. Clicked into this perspective, social media morphs from a relationship-buster into a potent tool—one that fosters communication, strengthens bonds, and narrates a digital saga humming with love, respect, and understanding.

As you cross tunnels of hashtags and newsfeeds, remember that the essence of a relationship lies not in the posts shared but in the feelings exchanged; not in the likes received but in the respect given. So, let social media be a canvas—a canvas that paints not an utopic illusion but a realistic picture of your journey. A journey that appreciates joys, braves storms, values respect, and above all, treasures love—the bond that holds together an essence that no 'like' can measure and no 'post' can define.

| FACING CYBERBULLYING AND DIGITAL ABUSE

When the digital realm is tarnished by the aggressive brushstrokes of cyberbullying—the cascading likes morph into scathing taunts, and familiar platforms feel like battlefields. Suddenly, you find yourself under an unwanted spotlight—criticized, belittled, or harassed—creating an echo chamber of negativity, fear, and anxiety.

Cyberbullying and digital abuse don't shy away from any corner of the online world. Social media channels, e-mails, gaming platforms, or chat forums—these digital specters lurk in all, suffering no bounds or limitations. A ruiner of reputations, framer of mental health issues, and a facilitator in relationships, cyberbullying escalates from mere online nuisance into real-world distress.

So how does one combat these cyberpunk shadows? For starters, recognition is cardinal—understanding what counts as cyberbullying—whether it's harmful comments, sharing inappropriate images or videos, or invasive hacking into personal accounts. Recognizing these red flags sketches the initial line of defense.

If you come under the crosshairs of cyberbullying, the foremost step is not to respond. Cyberbullies often seek a reaction, a validation of their power. Denying this in the form of silent strength often defuses their intent. Keep the evidence though before the silence—any harmful text, pictures, or accusations are necessary ammo in the fight against cyberbullying.

Next, block the bullies. Most digital platforms offer features to block, mute or report offensive individuals—use these weapons to your advantage. Cutting out the negativity shields you and reduces their reach, lowering their impact.

It's essential to report the bullying. Bring the incident to the platform's attention, contact your service provider, or in severe cases, alert the law enforcement. Just as bullies don't operate within bounds, legal aid in preventing cyberbullying isn't restrained either. Certain laws and regulations extend protection, advocating your right to online security.

An often overlooked yet incredibly potent support system is your close network of friends, family, or trusting acquaintances. Share the incident with them—don't let the embarrassment or fear make it a solitary battle. Vocalizing your ordeal not only aids mental comfort but also prepares you to deal with it better.

Yet, as much as we aim to guard ourselves from the assault, we should also ensure we aren't unintentionally perpetuating the cycle of abuse. Considerate online behavior is an individual and collective responsibility. Practicing empathy, respecting differences, and adhering to a code of digital ethics forges a healthier, friendly, and inclusive digital environment.

Remember, at its core, cyberbullying is a power play. Don't cower in fear, rather wear a shield of resilience, a cloak of intelligent choices, and arm yourself with assertiveness and confidence. Embrace the power of silence, the strength of reporting, and the energy of an empathetic network. Let these become your defense against the faceless bullies lurking in the digital shadows.

Moving forward, the dream is not just to clear out the cyberbullies but to create an atmosphere that doesn't incubate them in the first place—an online landscape that thrives on respect, understanding, and empathy instead of fear and negativity. And while this might seem like a Herculean task, remember that every respectful comment, every line of defense raised against a bully, and every supportive message sent to a victim, are all incremental steps towards this goal.

So, as you navigate the superhighways of the internet, remember you are not alone. Let not the occasional darkness blur your vision of the brighter digital pastures. Keep going forward, trusting that the screens will eventually clear, and the push of negativity will give way to the pull of positivity, respect, and safety. Blanketing all, a hope that our shared digital expanse will one day encapsulate an environment where respect overpowers bullying, understanding drowns abuse, and empathy echoes louder than any cyber harm.

| PROTECTING YOUR ONLINE PRESENCE

Strolling through the alleys of the digital world, every post you make, every photo you upload, every status update is a brick in your online presence structure—a digital persona that should be safeguarded as mindfully as your personal information.

Think of your online presence as a digital diary, narrating your virtual narrative to the world. With this perspective, conscious evaluation of what to include and what to omit from this diary becomes critical. Oversharing personal details or broadcasting every mundane bit could give away more than intended, often falling prey to privacy invasions, cyberstalking, identity theft, or online bullying.

Adopt a thought-listener. Prior to sharing or posting anything, pause, and listen to that internal dialogue. Question if the share aligns with your comfortable digital-self image, does it unintentionally reveal private information, will it leave a lasting footprint you're comfortable with? Answering these questions guides you to make informed digital decisions.

Privacy settings—your digital shield. Be familiar with them, frequently update them. Be it social sites, online shopping portals or cloud storage—these settings control who can view your content, follow your updates, or share your posts. Consider these settings as a personal gatekeeper, allowing in what's welcome and fending off the unwanted.

Another smart move is googling yourself. Documenting what kind of information, images, or discussions are available about you on the internet provides insight into your digital aura. With this knowledge, you can take proper steps, if required, to manage and protect your online presence.

A significant aspect often missed in online presence protection is digital hygiene—updating anti-virus software, keeping your operating system and applications updated, and using robust, unique passwords across platforms. Just as you would lock your home when you leave, so too should your digital domicile be secured.

In the end, protecting your online presence isn't a one-time cybersecurity drill—it's an ongoing journey of maintaining digital health. Each share, each post, each interaction contributes to your digital identity. Ensuring the journey aligns with a path of privacy consciousness, respect, and empathy positions you better in the global digital village.

As you embark upon your digital journey, remember, you are the author of your online narrative. Wrapping it in a protection cover of privacy practices, conscious sharing, respect for others, and regular check-ins will ensure it reflects a tale that is authentic, respectful, and most importantly, safe. Sailing smoothly in the digital sea is not just about steering clear of the storms, but also about wisely navigating through the calm. So, let the compass of digital wisdom guide you to protect your online presence—a shield that in turn protects you.

CHAPTER 9
DECODING PORNOGRAPHY

| NAVIGATING THE REALM OF DIGITAL DESIRE

In our digital age, the realm of desire has found a virtual niche—the domain of pornography. Offering anonymous, on-demand access, the world of pornography can often be the gatekeeping exploration of desire for many. Yet, its neon signs are illuminated not just by adult entertainment but also by cardinal questions—

questions that tackle ideas of consent, illusion versus reality debate, implications on body image, and potential impacts on relationships.

Approaching this digital landscape of desire, it's crucial to remember that the viewscape is not merely an exploration of sexual curiosity but a scope of examining the very understanding of sexuality and relationships. It is vital, therefore, to be equipped with accurate information, a critical understanding, and a priority for your physical and emotional well-being as you navigate through this digital desire domain.

And it commences with consideration. Consumption of explicit content isn't merely a reflection of curiosity or desire; it potentially lays digital footprints that warrant keen consideration. Questions as innocuous as what site to visit can hold significant implications— illegal content, potential exposure to malware, or violation of privacy protocols. A single click here, far from just igniting curiosity, could ripple into legal concerns or unwanted digital repercussions.

Further, the understanding that explicit content majorly thrives on creating fantasies—fantasies that might color the sexual script but rarely mirror reality—is paramount. Understanding where real-life courses and pornographic scripts divert helps craft a more informed, realistic perspective towards sex. Recognizing that porn's portrayal of immediate arousal, lack of explicit consent, or climactic expectations don't often echo real-life sexual dynamics assists in separating the fictional reel from the reality.

One of the fundamental navigational aids in this exploratory journey comprises open, honest conversations—conversations that voice concerns, debunk myths, and facilitate a balanced understanding. Be it seeking authentic sexual information, discussing the potential impacts of pornography, or sharing related anxieties—a respectful, non-judgmental conversation opens avenues for clarity and reassurance.

Entering the realm of pornography isn't a single-player game—it echoes in the dynamics of a relationship. Navigating the difference between personal consumption and shared exploration, discussing comfort zones, respecting boundaries, and understanding its potential impact on sexual expectations—these are signposts that inform a mindful journey.

Finally, recognize the importance of control in this digital exploration. Like any form of media consumption, pornography viewing needs a check—a check on time spent, content consumed, and the potential emotional impact. Recognizing signs of overreliance, adverse effects on personal life or relationships, and seeking help when needed is a pledge of self-care that values well-being over exploration.

Navigating the realm of digital desire, remember, is not about surrendering to a flood of fantasies but about sailing with the anchor of knowledge, compass of understanding, and the map of self-awareness. Stitching these navigational aids, we embark on a journey—not just of exploring desires but of a dialogue keen on understanding, a perspective enriched with reality, and a self-awareness safeguarded with well-being.

In the end—whether it's the climax of a scene or the seal of a cursor— the interplay of sexual exploration and pornography is a personal narrative. A narrative carved not just by the glow of a screen but the echo of understanding, the reflection of self-awareness, and the silhouette of respect—for self and others. That's the art of navigating the realm of digital desire—the art of crafting your understanding and writing an informed narrative of exploration.

REALITY VS. FANTASY:
THE EFFECTS OF PORN ON PERCEPTION

In the labyrinth of desires, the kingdom of pornography holds a peculiar allure. A world inscribed in coded fantasies, where exaggerated scripts meet exaggerated bodies, where the reel-linear trail concludes invariably with heightened pleasure—a world that weaves a patchwork quilt of fantasies. Steps away from reality, these fantasies whip a tempest that can potentially blur the lines between reality and fiction, leading to skewed perceptions and implications.

Shaped by the spectacle of fantasy, the untamed currents of pornography propose a hyperbolic mirror to authentic sexual interactions. It teases instant arousal, advocates theatrics of pleasure, and builds on tropes of dominance and submission—all choreographed to the melody of intuition, with virtually minimal script of explicit consent or emotional connection. These elements steer into a deeply sexualized narrative—but a narrative far detached from the holistic wheel of actual intimate exchanges.

The pleasurable illusion, on the digital screen, is not merely an assembly of acts—it's a magnetic pull that can subtly morph perceptions about sex, about bodies, about relationships. As users, particularly those venturing into their initial contact with sexual exploration, consume these collages of fantasies, their understanding of sex—its dynamics, its expectations, bodies, and roles—can inadvertently color from the pallete porn prescribes.

Impacted, the awareness that real-life sexuality dances not just to the erotic beat but also to the rhythm of respect, consent, and emotional connection can find itself lost in the noise of amplified fantasies. Naïveté or lack of balanced sexual education can lead users, especially teens, down the lane believing pornography as the roadmap for sexual behavior—a roadmap more likely to derail than guide accurately amid the trenches of intimate relationships.

There might bloom a shadow across self-esteem and body image. As the hypersexualized, often objectified bodies—airbrushed to perfection, skilled in desire, devoid of flaws —bequeath new standards of beauty, the comparison to these glorified figures might sow seeds of self-doubt and insecurity. The chase to act, to look, to satisfy like the silver screen models, can root a tree of dissatisfaction blotting out the radiance of self-love and acceptance.

Similarly, the porn-script marked by instant sizzle and climactic ecstasy, with little space for the gradual flame of desire or the vulnerability of sexual uncertainty, can invite unrealistic expectations. The anticipation that real-life intimacy should mimic pornographic performance or pleasure can lead to anxiety, dissatisfaction, or intimacy rifts.

Yet, amid these effects, two potent tools can script the check and balance—education and communication. An understanding of what pornography is—an adult industry product designed for fantasy, not a subject for "Sex 101". An understanding that the human body is diverse and beautiful in reality, not a photoshopped canvas. An understanding that intimacy thrives upon consent, communication, understanding, mutual satisfaction—a spectrum that embraces the imperfections, the vulnerabilities, the slow journey of desire.

These points of understanding align the compass back to reality— the reality that intimacies are complex, bodies are unique, respect is fundamental, and sex can be clumsy, intimate, passionate, slow—far from the glamorous montage porn projects. This balance between fantasy consumption and reality acknowledgment paves the way towards a healthy perspective—not just of viewing pornography but also of fostering a balanced understanding of one's sexuality and relationships.

In the end, the screen chronicles a fantasy—the pulsating heart navigates the reality. And it's the rhythm of that beating heart, guided by the melody of respect, consent, communication, and self-esteem that conjures the symphony of an enriching sexual narrative. A narrative that steps out of the shadow of fantasy to bathe in the sunlit reality—a reality rooted in the understanding that true intimacy encompasses more than just the physical; it weaves in the emotional, nests in the mental, and flourishes in mutual respect and love. Illusions may set the screen afire—the reality, however, ignites the heart.

| PORNOGRAPHY'S ECHO IN RELATIONSHIPS

Sparking curiosity, fueled by desire, and seeping into the intimate corners, pornography unceasingly ripples through our relationships. Whether as a shared pursuit or a harbored secret, it forces a challenge—how to navigate the explicit undercurrents without allowing them to corrode the shorelines of the relationship tapestry.

Pornography presents a dual face, a Janus of the digital age. On one hand, it can be a space of common exploration, an aphrodisiac igniting conversations about desires, spurring sexual exploration, providing a spark for intimacy in a relationship. It can propel fantasies, lead to awareness of kinks or appeals—breathe a hedonic oxygen into the relationship tapestry.

Yet, the alter face of this Janus isn't as bedazzled. Unregulated use, divergent comfort zones, unrealistic expectations—these crypts can subtly yawn open, echoing potential strife in the relationship dynamics. The areas of concern are manifold—skewed sexual expectations, desensitization towards partner, body image issues, anxiety over performance, or appetite for more extreme content—each a potential pitfall.

At the helm, it's crucial to note that pornography doesn't paint an accurate script of healthy sexual relations—its creative liberty omits the fundamentals of respect, consent, emotional connection. These nuanced layers, often erased in the consumable packaging of porn fantasies, are the pillars on which fruitful relationships rest. Decoding this difference between the reel of porn and the real of relationships is a foundational step.

A needle of contention often threading through relationships pertains to the frequency, content, and intention of pornography consumption. Does it chip away at shared intimacy or quality time? Does the narration steer towards disrespectful or non-consensual content? Are shared sexual encounters morphing to echo porn-like performance? These are alarm bells hinting towards a needed conversation—understanding that pornography is a commercial production, and its glamour-studded, fast-paced plot might not necessarily translate well into real-life scenarios.

Navigating these concerns carves a path to an essential fulcrum in relationships—communication. Open, honest conversations about the role and impact of pornography use can steer the relationship ship towards calmer waters. Expressing comfort levels, establishing boundaries, discussing issues, and potential solutions—all these are navigational aids in the voyage of understanding pornography's echo in relationships.

Acceptance that partners may have different perspectives or comfort levels with respect to pornography use fosters respect. A willingness to adjust and find a mutually equitable solution nurtures the relationship root. A commitment to keep the lines of communication open and fluid invests in relationship health.

In the grayscale of pornography's relationship hue, the keyword is balance. A balance between individual desires and shared intimacy, a balance between exploring sexual curiosity and fostering emotional connection, a balance between silent acceptance and shouted confrontation.

As the conversations navigate these complex currents, another facet often overlooked is the role of sex education. A comprehensive understanding of respectful, consensual, realistic sex plays a versatile role—not just in bridging the pornography-reality gap but in fostering open, informed dialogues, thereby strengthening the relationship dynamics.

In conclusion, the echo of pornography in relationships—whether a resonating harmony or a dissonant note—largely amplifies based on how the frequencies are tuned. Balancing the tune with open dialogue, mutual respect, comprehensive sex education, and realistic expectations can potentially morph the dissonance into a harmony—a harmony that doesn't shroud in the silence of judgement or scream in the chaos of unmanaged conflicts, but resonates in the calmness of understanding—the understanding of self, the partner, and the relationship dynamics.

And in this understanding echoes an echo that not just navigates the ripples of pornography but feeds into the fabric of the relationship—a fabric that weaves threads of respect, consent, communication, emotional connection—a fabric where the echoes of shared bonds, shared respect outshine any cultural, digital, or societal noise—a narrative where the harmony of understanding harks louder than any dissonance. That's the codex of decoding pornography's echo in relationships—the harmony of understanding, the symphony of shared respect, the melody of mutual trust.

| APPROACHING THE CONVERSATION ABOUT PORN

In the grand theater of relationships and sexuality, pornography often treads the stage as a shadow character—visible yet silent, present, yet shrouded, influential, yet unaddressed. Nudging this character into the spotlight requires an artful direction of communication—the art of approaching the conversation about porn.

Yet, as daunting as this curtain-raiser might seem, the stage settles into an engaging dialogue with a thoughtful mix of respect, understanding, and openness. Setting off on this conversational voyage, the compass that guides is empathy—for oneself and for the significant other.

Preparation forms the foundation of an effective dialogue. Being poised for different reactions, equipped with basic knowledge about pornography's pros and cons, understanding its potential impacts on oneself, the partner, and the relationship—these form the tangible bricks of this foundation. It anchors the conversation with factual information, minimizing chances of uninformed comments or misconceived arguments.

Next, in this theatrical dialogue, timing assumes a star role. Ensuring the conversation surfaces at a peaceful, private, and comfortable setting invites a conducive atmosphere for open conversation. A rushed intermission, a public audience, or a tense ambiance can quickly flip the script from a compassionate dialogue to an acute confrontation.

Door to the dialogue opened, focus on expressing self-perceptions, expectations, concerns regarding pornography. The 'I' statements can direct this expression without hurling accusations—saying 'I feel...' instead of 'You always...'. This approach preserves dignity, nurtures respect, and fosters a receptive atmosphere for the conversation.

Listening—with an empathic ear and an open mind—echoes as pivotal in this conversation. Welcome differing perspectives, accommodate silence, ponder over the reactions, and most importantly, ensure validation of the partner's feelings. This welcoming stance not only cements mutual respect but also encourages honest sharing.

The dialogue on pornography isn't a one-act criticism but a recurring play. Relationship dynamics shift, perspectives evolve, comfort zones alter—a continual space for conversation prevents the narrative from falling into static silence. Recognizing the process as ongoing, engaging in frequent check-ins underlines commitment to mutual understanding and relationship wellbeing.

Finally, recognize that this conversation is likely a branch of a grander dialogue—of sex, of intimacy, of acceptance. Exploring these core themes nestling the specific topic of pornography might bring to surface deeper insights, better understanding, and an enriched relationship fabric.

Guiding this narrative of understanding, remember, the conversation lights not simply to navigate the currents of pornography. It shines a spotlight on understanding partner perceptions, fostering shared respect, bridging knowledge gaps, and exploring intimate dynamics. It distills an essence that adds not just to navigating pornography but steering through the broad ocean of relationship communication.

Such a conversation—whether concluded in shared laughter or a contemplative silence, whether ending in an agreement or a respectful disagreement—stiches yet another empathetic pattern into the shared relationship tapestry. A pattern that echoes understanding, respect, open dialogue—a pattern unveiling not just a conversation about pornography but about bonding threads of shared intimacy, educated choices, and mutual respect. In the grand theater of relationships, this conversation underscores not a mere dialogue, but a narrative of shared understanding, respect-filled communication, and resilient connection—a narrative that enriches the broader canvas of relationship dynamics. And that's the quintessential art of approaching the conversation about porn—a canvas, a narrative, a dialogue that enriches the broader relationship theater.

| SEEKING SUPPORT AND INFORMATION

The digital highway of pornography, as alluring as it may seem, is fraught with intriguing bends and tricky potholes. It spins a fantastic narrative but momentarily blurs the line where reality ends and fantasy begins. Hence, embarking on this journey becomes a more enriching and safe experience when complemented with a network of support and armamentarium of accurate information.

While pornography's medium is primarily digital, support and information sources extend beyond the digital domain. They bloom from professional counsellors, healthcare providers, educators, trusted adults to reliable online resources. They shape a compass that not only navigates the pornographic landscape but also the broader territory of sexual health, relationship dynamics, and self-esteem.

Professional counsellors, therapists, or sex-education specialists serve as a reservoir of reliable information, guidance, and support. They can help unwrap the complexities, debunk the myths, address doubts or concerns, and counsel about healthy sexual attitudes. They underscore the importance of pornography's demystification from a sheer tool of arousal to a commercial product laced with fantasy.

Educators—be it school-based or community educators—bear potential to foster a credible environment where candid discussions about pornography, its impacts, and the conjoined web of sexual education flourishes. They contribute to a culture that respects curiosity yet regulates misinformation, that values open conversations yet demystifies fantasy.

Trusted adults—parents, relatives, family friends—offer a unique support system. They can transform potentially awkward conversations into nurturing dialogues, laying the ground for honest sharing and learning. Navigating queries, addressing concerns, encouraging informed outlook towards pornography—their understanding and availability can instill a sense of ease and openness among teenagers.

The expanse of the internet nestles a diversity of resources for seeking support and information. Websites dedicated to sex education, online forums for exploring queries, social media platforms vocal about sexual health—all are potential resources. They provide a vista of updated, authentic, and comprehensive information—addressing the natural, the taboo, the awkward comfortably.

However, it's crucial to ensure credibility when sourcing information online. Relying on websites that display transparency in terms of their sources, mission, or associated professionals is vital in avoiding misinformation traps. Equally important is respecting legality and the potential impact on digital footprints when surfing for information.

To cap all, remember, seeking support or information isn't indicative of weakness or embarrassment. It's a testament of strength, self-respect, and informed decision-making. The doorway to comprehensive knowledge about pornography isn't locked with a single key—it opens with various keys, each representing a different source of support and information.

Ultimately, these avenues of support and information propel a healthy, informed dialogue—not just about pornography but extending into the broader vista of personal boundaries, respect for self and others, and mutual consent. A dialogue that adds not just to circumnavigating the intricacies of pornography but to understanding its broader foothold in the sexual and relational landscape. A dialogue that pivots not on the axis of misinformation, judgment, or embarrassment but on the manifold dimensions of understanding, respect, and openness. And that's what seeking support and information ultimately fuels — an informed, respectful, and nuanced dialogue — a dialogue that propels the dialogue wheel not just for an individual but for society at large.

CHAPTER 10

THE RHYTHM OF RESPECT

| DEFINING RESPECT WITHIN RELATIONSHIPS

As the emotional fabric of relationships twirls and threads, one element tattoos its motif across the full tapestry—respect. Restrained by the misconception that it's common courtesy, mere politeness, the true depth of respect is routinely forgotten or misunderstood. Yet, when carefully observed, respect unfurls as the invisible conductor orchestrating the harmonious symphony of emotional exchange within relationships.

Every healthy relationship conducts this rhythm of respect—a rhythm that pulsates through varying tempos and notes, each echoing a defining principle or action. It's a rhythm that doesn't simply retain a constant beat, but fluctuates, adapting and evolving, stepping in sync with the dynamic dance of relationships.

Within the sphere of relationships, respect illuminates as conscious recognition and sincere appreciation of each partner's inherent worth. It sings the song of shared human dignity, acknowledging each individual as invaluable and irreplaceable. This intrinsic recognition stimulates a prism of respect—respect for each other's rights, feelings, experiences, thoughts, and traditions—each refractive shade contributing to the illuminating spectrum of a respectful relationship.

Moreover, respect reflects a deliberate alignment of actions and words, an alignment that resonates understanding and validation. It's not merely passively acknowledging the partner's perspective but actively integrating this understanding into behaviors, communications, and decisions. It's fostering an environment of inclusivity — an environment that gives room to accept and embrace differences, fostering a climate where unique identities are not crushed under the wheels of a singular narrative.

Respect threads a delicate yet firm bond of trust and safety within relationships. It manifests as honoring personal boundaries, not steaming through them, as dutiful confidentiality, not casual commentaries. Dignifying shared secrets, privatizing personal experiences mirror respect's reflection in a relationship's safety vault.

Yet another melody that respect hums in relationships is the patience of understanding—the patience to understand partner's viewpoints, emotions, or behaviors. Even when disagreements lead to discordant notes, respect fine-tunes the rhythm by replacing contempt with curiosity, judgement with empathy.

Respect's finest act in the relationship theater is perhaps acknowledging the partner's personal growth space. Appreciating that while partners share a common stage, each has a unique script of life—individual dreams to chase, personal battles to fight, and a solo path to self-discovery. Respect is ensuring this personal growth script isn't overshadowed by the relationship's shared narrative.

Last and far from least, a reverb of respect is expecting respect in return. It is valuing one's own feelings, rights, and needs, and embracing the conviction that one deserves respect as much as their partner. Respect, after all, is an emotional exchange—a mutual melody, a shared dance, a partnered play.

It's important here to remember that respect isn't the glorified grandeur of romantic gestures or the high praise in public domains. It's the everyday acts—the listening ear, the patient conversation, the accepted disagreement, the honored boundary. It's the acts that might not shine under the spotlight but subtly weave respect's golden thread across the relationship tapestry. End of the day, respect may not command an encore applause, but it composes the symphony of a fulfilling, healthy relationship.

Unraveling this prismatic spectrum of respect helps paint a picture defining respect within relationships—an image that portrays respect not just as admiring sympathy or superficial courtesy, but as a complex amalgamation of sincere recognition, active validation, deliberate understanding, unwavering trust, patient acceptance, room for individual growth, and self-respect. An image that delineates respect to be not an optional accessory but a mandatory outfit in the relationship ensemble. An image that emphasizes that respect nurtures not only the roots of shared love but also the branches of mutual understanding, the blossoms of open communication, and the fruits of personal growth. Defining respect within relationships, then, becomes an art—the art of decoloring societal stereotypes, of highlighting true shades, of brushing distinct strokes, and of crafting a radiant masterpiece—the masterpiece of a respectful relationship.

| THE ART OF RESPECTFUL COMMUNICATION

As the heartbeats of relationships drum along, communication's rhythm underscores every beat. Woven intricately into this rhythm is the golden thread of respect, embroidering the art of respectful communication. Paralleling a gracefully choreographed dance or a harmonious orchestra, it thrives on understanding, sincerity, empathy, and patience — each a significant note in this symphony.

The beauty of communication lies not only in talking but just as profoundly in the art of listening. Respectful communication, at its foundation, is rooted in active listening—a devout, undistracted time where the chorus of our thoughts drowns in the music of our partner's words. Active listening becomes the frame that holds the art—processing words, acknowledging feelings, understanding nuances, all while silencing the urge to interrupt, to judge, to retaliate.

As the artistry proceeds, the brush of understanding strokes the canvas next. Across differing opinions or clashing perspectives, understanding scripts a chapter of patience, of resilience. It hushes the tempest of defensiveness and confrontations, stirs the calm winds of curiosity, interest, and empathy. It reframes disagreements as opportunities of learning, opportunities to understand our partner deeply.

Linguistic palette in hand, respectful communication colors its words with sincerity, accuracy, and kindness. Word choices can set the tone for how our conversations transcend—a snide remark, a sarcastic comeback, or an accusing statement can quickly stray the dialogue towards confrontation. In contrast, framing thoughts with "I" statements—discussing feelings in response to actions, instead of accusing can keep the conversation anchored in a respectful, open harbor.

A visible shade in this art is respecting dignity, both of oneself and the partner. Respecting dignity translates into avoiding character-hitting words, steering clear of belittling or demeaning comments. It means selecting words that build a bridge of respect, not a wall of shame, painting a mural of mutual respect, not a portrait of bruised ego.

Yet another lyrical note in the respectful communication symphony is the silence—periods of quiet communion where words cease, and understanding reigns. Not every query requires an immediate response; not every statement warrants an instant retort. At times, respectful communication demands an interval of silence, a few moments to process thoughts, to moderate reactions, to avoid instant emotional reflexes.

Pioneering transparency, this art also encourages honest expression of feelings and needs—whether voicing personal concerns, quests for solace, acts that discomfort, or desires for change. Expressing these with a gentle, crystal-clear transparent tone fosters an atmosphere of trust and understanding.

The finale of the artful narrative is the exploration of non-verbal cues in communication— recognizing the tone that inflects words, the silent language of body gestures, the hidden melody in pauses. Fostering this awareness opens a whole new dimension of respectful communication, fine-tuning it to the subtle crescendos and diminuendos in the ballet of relationships.

This intricately choreographed dance of respectful communication weaves unconscious, a step at a time, elevating relationships to a grand stage. And in the spotlight, the characters waltz, tango, or cha-cha—the dance style varying from time to time, situation to situation, person to person. Yet, amidst all these variations, one rhythm remains consistent—that of respect. Amidst the twirls, the turns, the tumbles, the rhythm of respect echoes—the rhythm that decides whether the dance culminates into a graceful performance or scatters into an awkward stumble.

In the art of relationships, then, respectful communication stands not as a mere decoration but as a pivotal element, a vibrant color running through the relationship's spectrum. Viewing through this prism unveils that respectful communication extends beyond mere words—it is about active listening, understanding, transparency, patience, dignity—it's an art that balances honesty with tactfulness, clear expression with empathetic comprehension. It is an art that sketches its magic on the canvas of relationships, adding an irreplaceable vibrancy to the masterpiece we call love and connection.

| RECOGNIZING RESPECT'S ABSENCE

In the dazzling display of relationships, the rhythm of respect can often be drowned by the loud percussions of passion, excitement, or novelty. However, the absence of this rhythm introduces a disharmony that can disrupt the euphoric symphony, creating subtle ripples that eventually morph into cataclysmic waves. Recognizing these subtle signs of respect's absence is as significant as understanding its presence.

The absence of respect often surfaces in the camouflaged attire of a disrespecting language. Verbal exchanges peppered with derogatory terms, unjust accusations, or contemptuous sarcasm hint towards a fading respect narrative. In these moments, words strike beyond surface-level arguments, sinking into the depths of personal dignity and self-worth.

Another telltale manifestation is the frequent trampling over personal boundaries. Respecting boundaries — be it emotional, physical, or social — is a cornerstone of a respectful relationship. Overstepping these, whether consciously or unintentionally, underscore a deep chasm where respect should have been.

At times, respect's absence mirrors in the cold, cruel face of manipulation or control. Dictating personal choices, influencing decisions, imposing beliefs — these signs dress in the cloak of concern but conceal a fundamental disrespect. They hint at an unbalanced power equation, one that is marred by manipulation and control, replacing personal agency and freedom with restricted choices.

The vacant seat of respect can also make its presence felt in dismissive behavior—the act of ignoring or invalidating feelings, experiences, or opinions. Dismissal indicates a fundamental lack of consideration and acknowledgment of the other person's experience. It paints the portrait of superiority and depreciates the shared communication canvas.

Respect's absence may glare through constant criticism, often layered with demeaning comparisons or hurtful judgments. It underlines a deficit of understanding, empathy, and acceptance, spinning a narrative of dissatisfaction that can significantly dampen self-esteem and confidence.

Sometimes, respect sinks into the background as indifference takes the center stage. Neglecting partner's needs, disregarding their efforts, or indifferent to their feelings—indifference is a subtle yet significant indicator of the absence of respect.

Last yet crucial, every echo of abuse—physical, emotional, or sexual—resonates the starkest absence of respect. It marks a grave violation of human dignity, rights, and love, underscoring an immediate need for help and intervention.

It's important to remember here that the shadow of respect's absence isn't confined to tumultuous arguments or heated confrontations. It often hides in everyday interactions—in overstepped boundaries, in depreciating language, in dismissive behaviors, in manipulative acts. Each incident may be a hint—a hint to introspect the respect narrative and re-orchestrate the respect rhythm.

Recognition of these signs, however discreet or glaring, is the first step towards creating a change. It sparks the embers of self-worth, amplifying the need for respect, and in turn, commences the journey towards seeking it. However, decoding these signs or confronting them might not always be effortless—it may require help, support, and loads of courage.

Navigating the rhythm of respect in relationships then involves recognizing its presence, its absence, and importantly, negotiating its threshold—insisting on its indispensable presence, standing against its absence, and striving towards weaving it into the relationship's narrative.

In essence, recognizing respect's absence doesn't merely spotlight the deficits of the relationship. It inflates the willingness to seek change, the courage to demand respect, and the power to build a relationship rooted in mutual respect and understanding. It uncovers not just a chapter of recognition in the relationship book, but a narrative of change—a narrative where the ledges of low respect transition into the landscapes of mutual understanding and shared dignity—a landscape where respect doesn't stand at the gates, but walks hand-in-hand offering a splendid view—a view of a resilient, emotionally enriching, respect-resonating relationship.

| BUILDING SELF-WORTH AND MUTUAL RESPECT

In the sprawling landscape of relationships, two distinctive peaks rise to redefine its skyline – self-worth and mutual respect. As intertwined as roots of an ancient tree, these attributes interplay, dancing in tandem to the music of personal growth and relationship enrichment.

Building self-worth, first and foremost, is a journey inward. It is unlocking the door to self-understanding, exploring the corridors of strengths, weaknesses, interests, values, and beliefs. Identifying these facets underscores the unique individuality, the invaluable human worth that extends beyond relationship status, social recognition, or external validation.

Self-worth is also nurtured by setting and honoring personal boundaries. They are invisible, yet imperative lines drawn in the sand of personal space and comfort. Defining these boundaries and asserting them in relationships intertwines respect with self-worth, cementing a foundation of mutual understanding and regard.

Fostering self-worth alternatively flourishes by cultivating self-compassion, a soothing antidote to relentless self-criticism or unattainable perfectionism. Embracing imperfections, acknowledging struggles, and meeting them with kindness pumps life-blood into self-worth's heart, catalyzing the rhythm of self-respect.

Equally essential in this building process is engaging in acts that invigorate the sense of self-worth. Pursuing hobbies, nurturing talents, achieving personal goals—these acts uncoil the rich tapestry of character strength and individual potential, simultaneously enhancing self-worth and emanating inner radiance.

Swinging from self-worth to mutual respect, the light casts upon the inherent connection between these peaks. Mutual respect begins where self-respect lays its roots. Embodying self-respect models the understanding and validation desired from the partner. It silently communicates that respect is non-negotiable—a binding thread in the relationship fabric.

Building upon self-respect, attentive listening stitches another patch to the mutual respect quilt in relationships. Active listening affirms the validity of the partner's perspectives, acknowledging their inherent right to voice opinions or emotions. And in this acknowledgment, the seeds of mutual respect find fertile ground.

An ally of active listening in this respect-building expedition is open, respectful communication. Enclosing thoughts within the velvet-lined box of respectful language, exercising honesty without inflicting undue hurt, extends a bridge connecting hearers to speakers and fostering a channel of mutual respect.

Stepping forward, accepting and respecting differences builds yet another layer in the pyramid of mutual respect. Embracing differences in perspectives, personalities, or choices enriches relationships' texture with diversity, breathing into them a refreshing resilience and dynamic vigor. Simultaneously, it reinforces the essence of mutual respect — an acceptance and appreciation of the 'otherness' of the partner.

In this mutual respect architecture, trust builds another key pillar. Keeping promises, respecting privacy, or staying honest, are bricks adding to the trust structure. These bricks, layered with the cement of respect, concoct a fortified cornerstone for respect-looming relationships.

Walking these intersecting paths of self-worth and mutual respect is a captivating dance in the relationship ballet—a dance where the steps of self-respect entwine with the twirls of mutual understanding, self-compassion flows into the river of empathetic listening, and self-validation cascades onto the waterfall of mutual recognition.

The dance's beauty lies not in its symmetry but in its adaptiveness. It's the dance of personal evolvement and relationship growth—a dance where every step paints a stroke on the canvases of self-worth and mutual respect, creating not just a relationship portrait but a mural of personal and relational growth. A mural narrating the story of intricate respect patterns and hues of personal worth—a narrative of the resounding rhythm of respect choreographed with the symphony of self-worth—a narrative creating a resonating harmony—one underlying intimate relationships, redefining their emotional landscape, and sculpting the masterpiece of love rooted in respect and sprawling with self-worth.

▎THE CULTURE OF RESPECTFUL RELATIONSHIPS

In the illustrative journey of relationships, the culture of respect is the invisible hand that draws the outlines, fills the colors, carves out the nuances, and brings the entire portrait to vivid life. It's not merely an occasional visitor, but a constant inhabitant, one that shapes every conversation, every interaction, every understanding, and every shared moment.

At the heart of the culture of respectful relationships resides the pulsating rhythm of mutual recognition. This rhythm reverberates the belief in inherent dignity and worth—the belief that each partner, with their unique concoction of feelings, experiences, strengths, and vulnerabilities, deserves ample space in the relational sphere. It validates the truth that respect is a two-sided coin—bestowing it on the partner while reaffirming it for oneself.

Emerging from this shared recognition is the language of respect. Expressed in words of kindness, understanding, comfort, or love, this language echoes within the chambers of open conversations and heartfelt messages. It tiptoes on the doors of patience, knocks on the windows of clarity, and echoes in the corridors of comfort.

But the culture of respect echoes not merely in eloquent words but also in silent gestures. It threads itself in the fabric of everyday actions—acknowledging efforts, validating feelings, honoring boundaries, and cherishing individuality. It polishes every corner of a relationship with the shine of empathy, creating a shared space for the dance of respect.

Dressed in the robes of honesty and commitment, the culture of respect invites trust into these shared spaces. By the candlelight of truthfulness, partners find their way through the maze of misunderstandings, miscommunications, or conflicts. With the torch of consistency, they nurture the seeds of reliable promises into the tree of shared trust.

A vital hue painting the culture canvas is that of openness - epitomizing freedom to voice opinions, to share emotions, to express desires without the curtain of fear or judgment swaying in between. Openness unfurls a sky where concerns transform into stars of understanding, where curiosity takes flight in the plane of respect.

And when these ceaseless respect-waves reach the shores of conflicts, they reshape them, shaping piles of disputes into sculptures of understanding and differences into arrays of enlightening revelations.

Basking in the warmth of such a culture, relationships bloom — bloom into beautiful gardens speckled with vibrant shades of shared respect, individual value, mutual understanding, and emotional connection. Respect no longer remains confined within the pages of moral education textbooks, but breathes liveliness into day-to-day interactions and experiences—a heartbeat that sustains the lifeline of relationships.

In essence, the culture of respectful relationships isn't centered around grand gestures, magical moments, or staged performances.

Instead, it unfolds in subtle expressions, everyday interactions, and shared spaces—spaces for love, spaces for understanding, spaces for connection. It ropes love and respect together, turning them from individual entities into a symbiotic entity, a harmonious blend—a blend that gives life to the symphony of the rhythm of respect.

CHAPTER 11

STANDING FIRM AGAINST PEER INFLUENCE

| UNDERSTANDING THE WEIGHT OF PEER INFLUENCE

I n the adolescent journey of self-discovery and self-definition, peer influence often emerges as the invisible tide — a force that shapes thoughts, molds actions, and directs choices. It throttles the engine of teenage life—steering its pathways, fueling its milestones, and navigating its curves. As one walks this labyrinthine journey, understanding the weight of peer influence becomes as essential as reading the compass to keep the navigation in hand.

Peer influence, in its very nature, is a double-edged sword—one that can cut pathways to personal growth or stamp footprints on treacherous territories. It's a kaleidoscope, showcasing diverse colors of influence, each reflecting a mirror image of shared experiences, collective decisions, and uniform thinking.

One of the most potent reflections from this influence kaleidoscope is the pressures of compliance—pressures that often wear the costumes of shared decisions or group consensus. They traipse along the corridors of adolescent life, whispering coded messages— messages that quietly shape the perspective of what's 'normal', what's 'acceptable', or even what's 'expected'.

Yet another influential highlight in the peer realm is the fear of rejections—both explicit and implicit—the fear that sidestepping from group decisions might spark the flame of rejection, making one an outcast amongst friends. This fear becomes a hidden puppeteer in the adolescence play, maneuvering thoughts and actions across the stage of peer influence.

In contrast, adhering to group decisions paints a quick sketch of fitting into societal norms, effortlessly sailing the social boat. These synchronized choices, while marking routes of unity and harmony, also shadow the paths of personal identity and individual decisions.

Meanwhile, peer influence extends its invisible tentacles into the fragile realm of self-esteem, often becoming a determinant of self-worth. The adolescent need for societal validation elevates peer opinions into mirrors mirroring self-image, self-value, and self-confidence.

Understanding the weight of peer influence, then, interlaces untangling this intricate web, deciphering its coded messages and unmasking its conscious and unconscious impacts. It involves acknowledging these invisible hands of influence, while simultaneously learning to strike a balance—balance between individual identity and societal influence, balance between personal opinions and group ideologies, balance between the desire to 'fit-in' and the wish to 'stand-out'.

It also encompasses self-reflection, the art of peeling layers to reveal contexts, triggers, and emotional responses attached to peer influence. It's about wages on the scales of self-esteem and group acceptance—understanding when these weights tilt towards self-disregard, when peer opinions overshadow personal truths.

Zooming into the weight of peer influence leads to an insightful revelation—while the force of this influence is undeniable, its power is malleable. Choreographing its energy along the melody of personal growth, individual decisions, and emotional wellbeing transforms peer influence from an imposing pressure into an insightful guide—a guide to navigate through the vast social seas of adolescence.

Comprehending the weight of peer influence, hence, is an investment. It injects resilience into teen minds, equipping them to manage pressures, filter out negatives, and incubate positives. It threads a string of self-confidence, aiding them to face the fierce tides of teen life, encouraging them to bead their unique pearls of decisions along the string. It instills the courage to say 'No', to maintain personal stances, to fight against torrents, and to steer the ship of life across the ocean of adolescence, riding its high tides, enjoying its peaceful currents, and discovering their own distinct coastline of self-identity.

TACTICS FOR MAINTAINING YOUR STANCE

Navigating through the tumultuous seas of adolescence, one often sails against the gales of peer influence. While understanding the ebb and flow of this influence provides a compass, adopting tactics to maintain personal stance becomes the reliable oar, helping teenagers steer firmly towards their individuality and personal growth.

To begin with, the tactic of 'Assertive Communication' emerges as an effective lifeboat, enabling individuals to voice their opinions, beliefs, or concerns openly and confidently. But instead of firing a volley of defensive statements, assertiveness validates the right to personal standpoints, crafting articulate messages that convey the 'I' perspective, rather than launching accusations or counter-arguments

Following closely is the tactic of 'Effective Refusal'. Often, adamant refusals or blunt declines trigger confrontations or feed the flames of argument. Personal stance could be successfully maintained by opting for a tactful, polite, yet firm refusal. This should be combined with an ability to provide logical reasoning or alternatives, cushioning the impact of 'No' and retaining the command of personal stance.

Stepping forward, 'Self-Validation' evolves as a powerful psychological anchor, one which roots personal stance securely amidst the strong winds of peer pressure. Rather than outsourcing validation and self-worth to external approvers, drawing it from within provides a robust sense of self-confidence, ultimately fostering the capability to withstand the trials of influence.

Aiding on this journey, the tactic of 'Choosing the Right Company' surfaces as a beacon of emotional safety. Flourishing around like-minded peers or those who respect individual preferences nurtures a viable social environment, allowing teenagers to enjoy the camaraderie of friendship without forsaking their personal standpoints.

Further on, 'Practicing Mindfulness' weaves another strategic thread into this tactical tapestry. Mindfulness attunes individuals to their thoughts, emotions, values, and reactions, enabling a more attuned response to influence. It steadily steers away from impulsive conformity while aligning actions with personal values and choices.

Lastly, but significantly, 'Seeking Support' constitutes a crucial pillar of this tactical construct. Support could arrive as trusted adults, guidance counselors, or professional therapists. Accessing these support networks provides a platform to express concerns, seek advice, face challenges, and reinforce personal stances. It instills a sense of reassurance, a layer of protection against the winds of influence.

Weaving these together, these strategies serve as the unseen shield, a reservoir of strength, a repertoire of resilience against the tide of peer influence. They empower teenagers, not just as navigators of personal decisions, but as captains of their life voyages, orchestrating the harmony of peer interaction and independence. Under this tactical guidance, teenagers cultivate the courage to maintain their personal stance, the will to define their relationship with influence, and the inspiration to burgeon into trusted emotional navigators.

There's beauty in walking this path — a beauty that unfolds as we travel from the peaks of influence to the valleys of personal stance, serenading the dance of emotional strength and relationship dynamics. It's a journey of growing up, of harmonizing individuality with social interaction, of striking the rhythmic balance between the individual 'I' and the collective 'We'. It's here, in the interplay of influence and stance, under the narrative of individual strength, that the symphony of adolescence hits the most resonant note. Thus, emerges the poised, self-respecting teenager — a navigator and the captain of his journey, steering his ship in the vast seas of influence to the serene shores of identity, values, and independence.

| FRIENDSHIP'S ROLE IN PERSONAL DECISIONS

At the intersection of personal growth and societal interactions, friendship pulsates as a pivotal social sphere—a sphere where the kaleidoscope of personal decisions finds its dynamic playground, a sphere encapsulating the shared joys and sorrows, triumphs and challenges, experiences and adventures, growth and resilience.

The canvas of friendship, vibrant with distinct strokes, etches deeply into the process of personal decision-making, often serving as the unseen compass guiding the trajectory of choices. A friend's trust, their understanding, and shared experiences frequently provide the foundation upon which personal decisions find their footing.

By and large, friends serve as the sounding boards of our innermost thoughts, emotions, ideas, aspirations, and apprehensions. In exploring their viewpoints, feelings, and experiences, we confront alternate perspectives, challenge our preconceptions and broaden our understanding, thereby providing a richer substrate for informed personal decisions.

Alternatively, the cathartic process of sharing dreams, aspirations, or fears with trusted friends breathes life into personal decisions. These shared moments, brimming with empathy, support, and camaraderie, infuse decisions with emotional validation, causing shifts from internal debate to decisive action.

Friends often emerge as the mirror, reflecting an unfiltered image of ourselves, revealing blind spots, and helping us realize our authentic potential. They act as a catalyst, pushing us to introspect, evaluate, and transform our thoughts into action. Amidst the fluttering sails of peer relations, personal decisions find their wind in trusted friendships.

Conversely, friendships also stand as mighty fortresses against the winds of unwelcome influence. Amongst true friends, maintaining personal stance and exerting individuality don't rock the boat but stabilize it. It's within this harbor, safely anchored on respect for individuality, we can sail freely, navigated by our compass of personal decisions.

However, discerning the silhouettes of true friendship from the shadows of mere acquaintances or influence manipulators is critical. Friends who respect individual choices and acknowledge personal boundaries enhance decision-making confidence and empower stance maintenance.

Similarly, friends who offer honest, constructive feedback without the urge to sway decisions elevate the quality of personal choices. Their appreciative criticism promotes individual growth, resilience, and empowers values-based, well-informed decision-making.

Further, the power of friendship extends into the realm of emotional wellbeing, offering the resilience to withstand personal challenges or setbacks. The anchor of friendship steadies the ship of adolescence amidst the stormy seas of difficult decisions, providing emotional succor and resilience support.

Interestingly, true friendships illuminate the paths to not only what we can be but also, importantly, who we want to be. Friends, in their actions, words, and conduct, often serve as role models, subtly guiding and influencing personal decisions regarding character building, ethical standpoints, and life choices.

Now, navigating the depths of this friendship-ocean requires the oar of wisdom—the wisdom to discern, the wisdom to draw boundaries, the wisdom to choose. It involves finding the right tribe, maintaining personal stance amidst the tribe, letting positivity in while filtering out negatives, and, importantly, letting the essence of friendship seep into the bloodstream of personal decisions.

Friendship, thus, shines not only on the diary pages of shared moments and secrets but also profoundly imprints on the evolution of personal decisions—an imprint manifesting as a compass, a fortress, a sounding board, or a beacon of inspiration.

In essence, nestled within the intertwined threads of peer relationships, the pearl of friendship emanates a warm glow on our voyage of personal decisions. It emerges as the seaworthy vessel guiding us through the sea storms of adolescence—sailing smoothly amidst calm tides, standing firm against tidal waves, and persistently navigating towards the horizon of maturity—a horizon painted with the hues of strong individuality, decisive power, and empowered personal choices.

EMBRACING YOUR POWER TO CHOOSE

Climbing the success ladder of adolescence, if each rung represented a unique challenge, the power to choose would undoubtedly adorn the top rung. Embracing the power to choose anchors the ship of personal decisions, enabling one to charter its course across the ebb and flow of peer influence, dock at the safe harbor of individual identity, and ultimately embark on the journey of individual empowerment.

Embracing the power to choose tunes the orchestra of personal decisions. It is the conductor's baton that guides individual choices, setting the rhythm of personal growth, and orchestrating the harmony of relationship dynamics. It serves as the architect of personal development and instills the robust confidence to be at the helm of one's life experiences.

Further, harnessing the power to choose illuminates the path towards independent thinking. It enables recognition and appreciation of personal thoughts, beliefs, and perspectives. Independent thought paves the way for critical thinking, encourages questioning, cultivates skepticism about ill-informed beliefs, and fosters curiosity to seek well-informed, respectful, and enlightened viewpoints.

In contrast, exercising the power to choose also implies the power to reject. It's okay to refuse an invitation that you sense might lead you astray, to resist a modified version of your identity sprinkled with peer-approved traits, or to avert the well-woven web of peer pressure. The power to refuse is a formidable shield, one that protects your treasures of individuality, self-respect, and personal values from the invading forces of unwanted influence.

Embracing the power to choose requires robust self-awareness. It involves being attentive to your own feelings and intuitive responses, recognizing personal interests, and acknowledging personal boundaries. It fuels the engine of introspection, encouraging adolescents to explore their inner landscape, identify innate values, and align decisions with these core principles and feelings.

Using this power, one also unveils the potential to change. Be it the power to change harmful habits, break away from toxic relationships, or alter unhealthy patterns, the power to choose arms one with the promising hope of change. It fosters adaptability, builds resilience and encourages personal growth.

Brandishing this power to choose notably translates into an active role in life. No longer are you a passive bystander watching life pass by, but a dynamic participant, engaging with experiences, steering relationships, choosing responses, and above all, authoring your life story.

Yet, an often-underestimated dimension of the power to choose lies within the realm of mistakes and learning. The opportunity to make wrong choices, endure consequences, and learn from those experiences adds invaluable pearls of wisdom to the necklace of personal growth. It is the rein that harnesses the horse of personal development, riding on the path of self-reflection, learning, and improvement.

Finally, but not least significantly, the power to choose blooms into the fragrant flower of autonomy—a state of independent decision-making, self-regulation, and personal freedom. It underpins the pillar of personal agency, promoting ownership of actions, acceptance of outcomes, and commitment to growth—in essence, navigating one's life journey.

Embracing the power to choose, therefore, marks a significant milestone on the adolescent roadmap—a point where the power to choose morphs into the power of self-realization, personal growth, and identity formation.

In the end, just as each wave that crashes against the shore leaves its mark, each choice made contributes to character formation, leaving an indelible imprint on one's growth narrative. As the string of choices weaves the tapestry of life, it's the power to choose that holds the loom—crafting colorful patterns of unique personality traits, drawing the intricate design of personal identity, and painting the vibrant tableau of individuality. It's with this power that we emerge—the captains at the helm of our life, steering the vessel of adolescence amidst the thundering storm and soothing calm of the vast, expansive ocean of peer influence—into the serene harbor of resilience, growth, and self-reliance.

NAVIGATING LIFE'S CHOICES WITH CONFIDENCE

An unseen map lies etched onto the canvas of our lives—a map marked with the elaborate network of choices and decisions. As we chart our courses across this latticework of personal choices and peer influences, it's the compass of confidence that ensures steadfast navigation.

Confidence empowers us to anchor firmly in the sea of our beliefs, to weather the storm of external pressures, and to sail smoothly to the shores of personal identity and growth. It's the constant companion on our journey—a trusted guide that steers us past the turbulent waves of doubt and uncertainty.

Navigating life's choices with confidence begins with acknowledging our innate skills, strengths, and capacities. Recognizing these unique assets fuels faith in our abilities, harnessing the power to stand firm despite opposition, to choose to let our light shine amidst shadows of doubt, and to cultivate unwavering trust within oneself.

Next, confidence grows its solid roots in the fertile soil of self-awareness—an empathetic understanding of our needs, desires, beliefs, and values. With each choice we make based on this self-understanding, we trace a stroke on the portrait of our authentic selves—vibrant, bold, and undeterred by fear of judgment.

Successes achieved and obstacles overcome water the lush garden of self-confidence. By celebrating wins, no matter how small and by overcoming challenges, no matter how formidable, we condition our minds to recognize our capabilities. This recognition arms us with a strengthened belief in ourselves to make informed decisions, propped up with persistent resilience and unwavering determination.

Yet, the game of life often throws challenges that lead to setbacks. Confidence lies not in the denial of these setbacks but in finding the strength to bounce back, to learn from experiences, and to rise again. It's in the embrace and acceptance of these teaching moments that we brew the potion of unshakeable self-trust and optimism.

Importantly, true confidence lies in acknowledging our unique path, which does not need to conform to societal norms or expectations. This involves respecting our timeline of experiences, learning, growth, and decision-making. It means rejecting the notion of a one-size-fits-all life and embracing the idea of an individualized journey tailored to our desires, capabilities, and vision.

Finally, amid the whirlpool of life choices, confidence is a buoy of hope. It floats upon the tides of uncertainty, guiding our path, shining the light on opportunities, anchoring our decisions, and allowing us to swim through the currents of life.

Navigating life's choices with confidence, therefore, equips us to take charge of our experiences, to stand firm in our decisions, and to carve a unique path in the vast terrain of life. With surefooted steps and a clear gaze, we journey onwards, holding the torch of confidence high and paving the way for a bright future etched with the wisdom of our choices, the strength of our stance, and the integrity of our thoughts. Embrace your confidence — it is your compass in the journey of life choices.

CHAPTER 12

FORWARD THINKING: ASPIRING AND ACHIEVING

GOAL SETTING FOR PERSONAL AND RELATIONSHIP GROWTH

The voyage of personal and relationship growth meanders through the vibrant landscapes of adolescence, threading along the intertwined pathways of self-awareness, emotional maturity, and interpersonal skills. Goal setting appears as the indispensable compass on this journey—an instrument guiding individuals towards their aspirations, charting their routes, and bringing their dreams into the realm of reality.

At the core of goal setting for personal and relationship growth lies self-exploration—the journey of uncovering individual interests, identifying personal values, and recognizing areas of growth. It's in the embrace of this self-realization that meaningful and effective goals are born. Goals specific to individual needs take seed, germinate, and bloom into beautiful chapters of personal development.

Next, the process of setting personal and relationship goals calls for the spirit of adaptability. It's the strength to steer against the winds of uncertainty, cope with unanticipated situations, and redefine the course as necessary. Herein, goals become the dynamic guidebooks rather than rigid commandments—flexible to evolve with changing circumstances, learning, and growth.

However, the essence of setting attainable, realistic goals should underpin personal and relationship growth. Having the vision to strive toward long-term goals while concurrently celebrating each achievable small-step goal fuels motivation and strengthens the resolve to carry on. It's in appreciating these manageable milestones that the daunting summit of a long-term target becomes achievable and less intimidating.

Once defined, each goal nestles within the fortress of intentional actions and dedicated efforts. It is consistency—the discipline to maintain focus and the determined pursuit of planned actions—that transforms nebulous dreams into tangible achievements. Goals become the breeding ground for fostering responsibility, enhancing focus, and nurturing diligence—components that catalyze personal and relationship maturation.

Applying this to the realm of relationship growth opens avenues of interpersonal understanding and emotional intelligence.

Establishing goals to listen more, express emotions effectively, respect individual boundaries, and solve conflicts logically can elevate the quality of relationships, fostering deeper intimacy and mutual respect.

Importantly, embedding compassionate flexibility within these goals sets the foundation for healthy relationship dynamics. This denotes the practice of being patient with self and others, understanding the uniqueness of individual journeys, and adapting expectations in tandem with evolving growth and changing circumstances.

Finally, incorporating reflective feedback cycles in goal setting is quintessential. This involves assessing progress, analyzing obstacles, learning from setbacks, and tweaking future steps as necessary. The spirit of self-reflection births the wisdom of change—cultivating a sense of self-accountability, encouraging emotional balance, and channeling personal progress.

Doorways to the potential of personal growth swing open through goal setting. Every imparted lesson colors each threshold with hues of wisdom and resilience, enriching the tapestry of adolescent life. Meanwhile, relationship goals bring vibrancy to the canvas of interaction, etching in vivid strokes of emotional intelligence, mutual respect, depth of connection, and relational satisfaction.

Therefore, goal setting, with its ripple of beneficial impacts, aids in personal and relationship growth—a metamorphosis from the cocoon of adolescence struggles into the soaring butterfly of mature adulthood. Aligned with consistency, adaptability, realism, and reflection, it becomes the secret ingredient in the recipe of personal and relationship growth, culminating into a dish savored with the taste of success, fulfillment, and self-satisfaction.

| RELATIONSHIP BALANCE AND PERSONAL AMBITIONS

The journey of adolescence weaves a vibrant tapestry of intermingled threads representing personal ambitions and relationship balances. Striking a harmonious balance between the two is akin to an intricate balancing act—a dynamic equilibrium teetering between the pursuit of individual aspirations and the nurturing of interpersonal connections.

Personal ambitions, the fiery torches that light the path towards our potential, drive us forward in our lives. They shape our pursuits, our vision, and our direction. They serve as the fuel powering the engine of personal growth and accomplishment, representing our deepest desires, the highest peaks of our potential, and the promising horizons of our passions.

Simultaneously, the diverse relationships we foster—be it friendships, family bonds, or romantic affiliations—unfurl as the constellations guiding us through the dark expanse of our life's journey. They infuse our paths with shared joys, mutual support, companionship, and collective growth, each relationship a unique star illuminating our life.

Bridging these two facets—personal ambitions and relationship balance—involves harnessing the principle of mutual respect and understanding. Herein, recognizing the significance of both in shaping a wholesome, fulfilling life resonates as a crucial first step. It entails valuing personal aspirations while equally cherishing the role of meaningful relationships in our lives.

Appreciating personal goals and ambitions as integral to self-identity, self-growth, and personal fulfilment, it's vital to pursue these with steadfast focus and unwavering dedication. Simultaneously, strengthening the fortress of relationships necessitates an understanding of shared spaces, respect for mutual boundaries, and a reciprocal contribution to nurturing connection.

Creating a conducive environment where both personal ambitions and interpersonal relationships coexist harmoniously calls for open communication. Expressing personal aspirations, sharing dreams, elucidating challenges, and articulating needs—these components fuel healthy interactions and mutual understanding within relationships. They forge a bridge between the isle of individual dreams and the continent of social belonging, ensuring recourse for personal growth alongside the flourishing of relationships.

Further, fostering a balance invites the spirit of compromise and flexible adaptability. Sporadic sacrifices and adjustments for the benefit of relationships doesn't dwarf personal ambition but rather emphasizes the values of empathy, unity, and mutual respect. Likewise, leaning towards personal goals on occasion doesn't undermine relationships but instead instills a sense of purpose, self-empowerment, and personal growth.

Balancing personal ambitions with relationship dynamics also evokes the wisdom of time management. Essentially, it entails weaving a blend of 'Me', 'Us', and 'We' time—individual time for personal goals, one-on-one time with each connection, and collective time with the broader social circle. This approach nurtures the tree of personal goals while watering the roots of interpersonal relations, ensuring the concurrent flourishment of both.

Augmenting this balance, recognizing the exclusive journey of personal progress each individual undertakes builds bridges of understanding and support. Appreciating individual growth paths facilitates the co-existence of personal ambitions and relationship dynamics, ensuring neither overshadows the other.

In essence, the relationship balance and personal ambitions perform a harmonious ballet on the stage of adolescence—a dance orchestrated with the melodies of shared growth, solo performances, rhythmic understanding, and synchronized support.

Layered within this dance is the understanding that personal ambitions and relationship balance are not rivals within the pit of a competition. Instead, they are allies, complementary forces existing within the sphere of a fulfilled, enriched life. Personal ambition fuels the drive of individual growth, while relationship balances decorate the voyage with vibrant shades of love, unity, and shared experiences. Together, they sketch the evolving grandeur of adolescence, shaping the individual into a poised dancer on the stage of growth, aspirations, and connections, leading to an enriching performance of personal and social fulfillment.

| PREPARING FOR MATURE RELATIONSHIPS

As we traverse the cascading landscape of adolescence, nestled snugly in the winding trail ahead emerges the realm of mature relationships— a juncture where the turbulent rivers of adolescent relationships meet the serene ocean of adult interactions. Transitioning into this phase invites a tapestry of evolving emotions, broadening perspectives, deepening connections, and soaring self-growth.

Key to this transition is the pivotal role of self-awareness. This internal compass guides the journey of understanding personal emotions, acknowledging individual values, and recognizing personal boundaries. In cultivating a deep-seated knowledge and acceptance of one's identity, self-awareness infuses mature relationships with authenticity, personal integrity, and emotional depth.

Evolution towards mature relationships also requires embracing emotional intelligence— the ability to perceive, evaluate, and manage emotions, both personal and those of others. Herein lies empathy's nurturing role, promoting deeper understanding and fostering stronger connections. It empowers us to weave the threads of emotional understanding into the fabric of mature relationships.

Moreover, mature relationships thrive in the garden of effective communication— a lush space where thoughts and emotions bloom into shared understanding. It is this exchange of thoughts, clear expression of feelings, and open dialogue about needs, aspirations, and concerns that ensures a healthy, constructive, and growth-oriented relationship dynamic, bursting with shared experiences, mutual understanding, and collective growth.

Gazing upon the broad horizon of mature relationships, mutual respect shines as a beacon of thriving connection. Holding high the flag of personal boundaries, acknowledging differing viewpoints, and cherishing individuality, mutual respect foundationally underpins the landscape of mature relationships. Respect for another's journey, perspectives, and growth materializes a space of equality, acceptance, and trust.

With the dance of mature relationships, a rhythmic balance of independence and interdependence orchestrates the symphony of connection. Valuing personal space and individual growth harmoniously blends with the shared experience, mutual growth, and collective exploration. This equilibrium cultivates a relationship environment where personal growth coexists with the development of deep, meaningful bonds.

Intertwined in the journey towards mature relationships is the principle of active listening—the embodiment of respect, attentiveness, and understanding. Listening intently to another's narrative, acknowledging their sentiments, and valuing their perspectives— these facets of active listening contribute profoundly to the richness of mature connections.

Alongside, nurturing mature relationships envelops the act of giving and receiving—the shared exchange of support, care, and love. It fosters an environment of shared bonding and mutual nurturance, where each individual contributes to the relationship, reciprocally responsive to the other's emotional, intellectual, and relational needs.

On the flipside, mature relationships also invite the wisdom of conflict management. Navigating differences, managing disputes healthily, and expressing disagreements without harm form the pillars of mature conflict resolution—a cornerstone on the path of mature relationships. It fortifies the relationship structure, further fueled by solutions focus, flexibility, and reciprocal adjustments, lending resilience and sustainability to connections.

With maturity, accountability also seeps into the relationship fabric. Owning actions, accepting consequences, and rectifying mistakes paves the way for personal growth and relationship strengthening.

Anchored to a mature relationship's core, commitment helms the relationship vessel—a pledge towards the connection, resilience amidst challenges, and a sustainable bond. It paints the relationship canvas with strokes of trustworthiness, reliability, and enduring connection, birthing fortitude within the relationship bond.

In essence, preparing for mature relationships encompasses a transformative journey—one that refines raw emotions, broadens self-awareness, enriches communication, fuels emotional intelligence, and strengthens commitment. It nurtures the sapling of adolescent relationships into the mighty tree of adult connections, lush with the foliage of understanding, the blossoms of shared growth, and the fruits of lasting bond. This journey's culmination sketches a panorama of fulfilling, enriching mature relationships— a tapestry richly adorned with the vibrant hues of emotional maturity, the intricate patterns of understanding, and the exquisite embroidery of lasting connection.

| CONTINUAL GROWTH IN SEXUAL HEALTH KNOWLEDGE

With adolescence comes a blossoming of curiosity and an incessant pursuit to learn and grow. One field of life that continually shapes and influences this developmental stage is sexual health—a topic that demands lifelong learning, comprehension, and awareness. As ever-evolving beings in an ever-changing world, we are confronted with advancements in knowledge, shifts in societal norms, and progress in medical and scientific understanding. Embracing this flux in the realm of sexual health and committing to a path of continual growth in this knowledge transcends mere awareness—it signifies a conscious decision towards responsible health management, informed decisions, and holistic well-being.

At its root, a commitment to growing sexual health knowledge requires a shift in attitude—one that genuinely embraces learning, shuns ignorance, and actively seeks factual, scientific knowledge. This approach bolsters the capacity to critically examine information, question misconceptions, challenge stereotypes, and foster a deep-rooted understanding of sexual health.

Furthermore, the emphasis shifts from a one-time education to a life-long learning journey—an exploratory voyage that burrows deeper than mere surface knowledge. It welcomes an understanding of the physical aspects of reproductive health, delving into its emotional, psychological, social, and contextual dimensions. The breadth of this learning spans various subjects like consent, body image, STIs, pregnancy, contraception, menstruation, hormonal changes, and much more.

Linking this knowledge to real-world applications paints it with the hues of relevance and importance. This engagement with practical aspects—understanding the impact of decisions on personal health, recognizing issues and seeking professional help, responsibly managing relationships—nurtures an empowered individual who can stand firm in the face of uncertainty, misinformation, and societal pressure.

A commitment to the growth of sexual health knowledge also encompasses cultivating healthy, open dialogues about these topics. It breaks shackles of embarrassment and ignorance and normalizes discussions on tabooed aspects. It creates an environment conducive for adolescents to ask questions, seek reliable answers, and share their experiences without fear of judgment or ridicule.

Harnessing multiple sources of authentic and credible information plays a pivotal role here. Books like this one serve as reliable companions. However, benefiting from expert consultation, attending professional workshops, connecting with support services, and utilizing validated online resources also contribute to keeping this knowledge updated and thoroughly comprehensive.

Ultimately, an individual's continual growth in sexual health knowledge translates into growth in emotional maturity, cognitive understanding, and social responsibility. As this knowledge repository expands, it manifests in overall personal growth, enhanced self-awareness, and improved relationship dynamics. It enables adolescents to make informed decisions about their bodies, relationships, and lives in general—decisions echoed with respect, self-dignity, and an inherent understanding of personal boundaries.

Each footfall on the journey of continual growth in sexual health knowledge leaves an indelible imprint on the canvas of adolescence, coloring it with the hues of informed decisions, confident interactions, and healthy mindsets. And with each stride forward, an adolescent evolves—a caterpillar burgeons into a beautifully informed butterfly, equipped to navigate the expansive skies of sexual health, relationships, and personal empowerment. Such growth, with its rich tapestry of benefits, delivers more than knowledge; it unfurls the power that lies in being informed, responsible, and in control of one's own health and well-being. After all, knowledge is not just power—it's the key to freedom, self-awareness, and a fulfilling life.

▌ INSPIRING CHANGE AND EMPOWERMENT IN OTHERS

As we gain knowledge, grow in understanding, and strengthen our decision-making skills, we accumulate a wealth of valuable insights and influential potential. Like a river that gathers force from countless tributaries to shape the landscape it traverses, we, too, acquire the power to influence change, ignite inspiration, and instigate empowerment in others.

Embarking on this journey of change and empowerment commences with the ripple of self-awareness—a pebble dropped in the pond of existence, causing waves that gradually extend outward. As we grow in our understanding of our bodies, our emotions, our relationships, we arm ourselves with wisdom, which when shared, can enlighten and empower others navigating the murky waters of adolescence.

In igniting empowerment in others, compassion, empathy, and understanding stand strong as torchbearers. Empathy—lending an ear to listen, an understanding heart to feel, a comforting voice to console—echos sameness in experience, validates emotions, and imbues courage and strength. Such empathy morphs into a beacon for those who grapple with similar life phases, illuminating the darkened corridors of their progression.

Equally integral is the spirit of open communication. In advocating for honest discussions, challenging taboos, debunking myths, and addressing concerns, we transform erstwhile silences into informative dialogues. Unhindered conversations around complex subjects like sexual health, relationships, and body image contribute remarkably to enriching societal fabric, promoting understanding and fostering a community prevalent with respect, awareness, and acceptance.

A significant aspect of inspiring change and empowerment amalgamates the sharing of personal stories and experiences, the highs and lows, the challenges and triumphs. In doing so, we humanize our journey, offering an authentic peek into the maze of adolescence—an honest revelation encouraging others to embrace their narrative, fight their battles, and cherish their victories.

Passing the baton of knowledge, empowering the light of awareness, fostering courage, sowing seeds of confidence—these actions ripple out, birthing waves of change. Each person we lend a hand to, each friend we guide, each individual we inspire aesthetically contributes to changing the world—one person at a time.

However, a nuanced understanding of individuality must underscore such an endeavor. Recognizing that every personal journey is distinct, every pace different, and every experience unique aligns our inspirations with respect for individuality. It nurtures the roots of change and empowerment in a fertile soil of respect, patience, and understanding.

To inspire change in others is to create a symphony of empowered narratives. It is to shape a world enriched with informed individuals, capable of making conscious decisions about their bodies, relationships, and lives. It is to build bridges of understanding and acceptance between varied experiences, emotions, and struggles.

However, inspiring others far transcends shaping the world. It leaves a profound impact on our growth too—an imprint that colors our humanity, kindness, and respect for others. It fuels the river of our lives, adding vigor to its currents, depth to its flow, and richness to its essence.

Thus, inspiring change and empowering others erects the pillars of an empathetic, informed, and mature community—a society laced with wisdom, acceptance, and respect. We are guides on the labyrinthine path of adolescence and torchbearers lighting the way for others, shaping not just their journey but ours too. After all, change is contagious—Every ripple of inspiration we create can go on to create waves of enlightenment, empowerment, and evolution.

CONCLUSION

As we draw the closing lines of this illuminating journey, we take a moment to reflect on the chapters we've traversed, the insights we've gleaned, the revelations that have transformed our perspectives and, ultimately, the empowering wisdom we've gathered. We stand on the precipice of growth, our eyes marvelling at the expansive vista of knowledge we've charted. Like a butterfly that has emerged from a chrysalis of transformation, we, too, have undergone profound metamorphosis.

Over the course of these pages, we've explored the intricate facets of our beings—the body's transformation, intense emotional tides, the complex realm of relationships and the importance of sexual health education. Each nugget of wisdom teased from these studies paints a multidimensional portrait of the adolescent journey—a journey marked by glistening victories and hard-learned lessons.

Reflections and revelations have been our companions throughout, shedding light on the often-misunderstood aspects of adolescence, illuminating the path of personal growth, and unveiling the nuanced dynamics of relationships. Looking back, we appreciate these insights as catalysts, precipitating our evolution from the wellspring of curiosity to a river of understanding.

As we prepared for the future, we discovered the subtle dance between personal ambitions and relationship balance. We learned how to weave a harmony of autonomy and dependence, understanding the slight nudges of compromise, and the profound power of respect. Our understanding deepened about the necessity of setting reasonable goals. We found that in the heart of balance lies a thriving self-identity, preserved individuality, and flourishing relationships.

Our musings on mature relationships brought us face-to-face with the hallmarks of deeply meaningful and thriving connections— mutual respect, effective communication, emotional intelligence, and unshakeable commitment. Our eyes opened wider to the transformative power of understanding, acceptance, and heartfelt expression. And from this elevation, we gleaned the importance of growing and evolving together.

Each step of this journey nurtures us with confidence—an empowering sense of surety that lets us face the coming stages with fortitude. As you—the reader—prepare to step beyond these pages, trust that you do so armed with immense knowledge and secure in your ability to make informed decisions.

Moving forward, though the path may sometimes be shrouded in uncertainty, remember always that the torch of knowledge you now hold will undoubtedly dispel any lingering shadows. Your arsenal of understanding, enriched by the jewels of self-awareness, empathy, communication skills, and positive self-image, will invariably guide you through the complexities of adolescence and beyond.

Be assured that the wisdom you've gleaned from this book instills in you the power and confidence to navigate your personal life, manage relationships, and understand your body and its changes better. This newfound confidence, anchored firmly in knowledge, will signal your readiness to face challenges, to dare to ask questions, and to demand respect for your choices and boundaries.

Now armed with an understanding of the importance and consequences of your actions, you are ready to share this light, this powerful knowledge, and inspire others around you. Stand tall as an advocate for informed choices, feed the spark of awareness, stoke the flames of education, and light the path for those following in your steps.

Speak openly of what you've learned, dispel misunderstandings, spread the magic of open communication and instill empathy within your circles. Be the change you wish to see, challenge the norms that no longer serve you, and ardently pursue the path that resonates with your authentic self.

In essence, this enlightening voyage has opened a window to a new world of knowledge and understanding—a world where educated decisions replace uninformed choices, where open conversations break through the barriers of silence, and where self-worth stands undefeatable against societal pressures. As we delicately close this window, let the radiance of wisdom and understanding spill over, illuminating the path ahead.

Remember, each new day invites opportunities for growth, for learning, and for evolution. Each challenge presents a stage to embody what you've learned, each relationship a canvas to paint your understanding, and every experience a chance to cultivate your growth.

As this book illuminates the path, each of you—dear readers— become the torchbearers. Spread the light of knowledge, of understanding, of empathy, and of respect. And as this light disperses in the world, remember that not only have you grown from the process, but you are now inspiring growth in others. Therein lies your profound impact—a testament not just to the journey you've undertaken, but also to the incredible path that awaits each one of you. Carry this enlightenment within you as an enduring flame, a source of warmth, guidance, and empowerment that will illuminate your way, today and always.

Made in United States
Troutdale, OR
06/27/2024

20856739R00090